Scarecrow Film Score Guides
Series Editor: Kate Daubney

1. *Gabriel Yared's* The English Patient: *A Film Score Guide*, by Heather Laing. 2004.
2. *Danny Elfman's* Batman: *A Film Score Guide*, by Janet K. Halfyard. 2004.
3. *Ennio Morricone's* The Good, the Bad and the Ugly: *A Film Score Guide*, by Charles Leinberger. 2004.
4. *Louis and Bebe Barron's* Forbidden Planet: *A Film Score Guide*, by James Wierzbicki. 2005.
5. *Bernard Herrmann's* The Ghost and Mrs. Muir: *A Film Score Guide*, by David Cooper. 2005.
6. *Erich Wolfgang Korngold's* The Adventures of Robin Hood: *A Film Score Guide*, by Ben Winters. 2007.

Erich Wolfgang Korngold's
The Adventures of
Robin Hood

A Film Score Guide

Ben Winters

Scarecrow Film Score Guides, No. 6

The Scarecrow Press, Inc.
Lanham, Maryland • Toronto • Plymouth, UK
2007

SCARECROW PRESS, INC.

Published in the United States of America
by Scarecrow Press, Inc.
A wholly owned subsidiary of
The Rowman & Littlefield Publishing Group, Inc.
4501 Forbes Boulevard, Suite 200, Lanham, Maryland 20706
www.scarecrowpress.com

Estover Road
Plymouth PL6 7PY
United Kingdom

British Library Cataloguing in Publication Information Available

Library of Congress Cataloging-in-Publication Data
Winters, Ben, 1976–
  Erich Wolfgang Korngold's The adventures of Robin Hood : a film score
guide / Ben Winters.
    p. cm. — (Scarecrow film score guides ; no. 6)
  Includes bibliographical references (p.   ) and index.
  ISBN-13: 978-0-8108-5888-6 (pbk. : alk. paper)
  ISBN-10: 0-8108-5888-6 (pbk. : alk. paper)
  1. Korngold, Erich Wolfgang, 1897–1957. Adventures of Robin Hood.
  I. Title.
ML410.K7356W56 2007
781.5'42–dc22   2006029741

Manufactured in the United States of America.

For my sister, Susie

and

*my parents
Jan and Dave Winters*

CONTENTS

ILLUSTRATIONS

Examples

Tables

EDITOR'S FOREWORD

The Scarecrow series of Film Score Guides is dedicated to drawing together the variety of analytical practices and ideological approaches in film musicology for the purpose of studying individual scores. Much value has been drawn from case studies of film scoring practice in other film music texts, but these guides offer a substantial, wide-ranging and comprehensive study of a single score. Subjects are chosen for the series on the basis that they have become and are widely recognized as a benchmark for the way in which film music is composed and experienced, or because they represent a significant stage in the compositional development of an individual film composer. A guide explores the context of a score's composition through its place in the career of the composer and its relationship to the techniques of the composer. The context of the score in narrative and production terms is also considered, and readings of the film as a whole are discussed in order to situate in their filmic context the musical analyses which conclude the guide. Furthermore, although these guides focus on the score as written text, bringing forward often previously unknown details about the process of composition as they are manifested in the manuscript, analysis also includes exploration of the music as an aural text, for this is the first and, for most audiences, the only way in which they will experience the music of the film.

The issue of a benchmark in compositional technique is particularly apposite in the consideration of any score by Erich Wolfgang Korngold, and especially so given the comparatively early date of *The Adventures of Robin Hood* (1938) in relation to the evolution of Hollywood sound film scoring practice. Korngold, and his contemporary

Max Steiner, have come to be considered retrospectively as 'founding fathers' of many elements of this practice, and yet this evaluation of them generates a whole new set of assumptions which deserve critical scrutiny. The casual listener, moved by the richness of Korngold's orchestration and his melodic facility, might well consider that he imported 'a better class of music' from Europe to Hollywood at a time when its musical idioms were fragmented by both the influence of Broadway imports and a collective uncertainty among directors and producers about the role of music in mainstream dramatic films. Yet as Dr. Winters shows, this assumption of a pure high-art pedigree and the intact preservation of its authorial voice in the otherwise complex and many-handed system of production is a flawed one. In this volume we are invited to revisit all our assumptions about Korngold, and thus about how we experience what is regarded as some of the most classical of all Hollywood film music. Furthermore, in revisiting one of the most influential of scores, we must reconsider some of the most influential of ideas in film musicology: about reading, about structure, and about process.

This volume brings a fresh and insightful perspective to the evolution of a well-loved score for one of the great swashbuckling films, but it is written in such a way that whatever the reader's level of musical knowledge or understanding, there is much to be learned and understood about what part the music plays in capturing for all time the heroics of Robin Hood.

Dr. Kate Daubney
Series Editor

ACKNOWLEDGMENTS

All music quoted from *The Adventures of Robin Hood* and all material from the USC Warner Bros. Archives, School of Cinematic Arts, University of Southern California, Los Angeles, CA 90089-2211 is by kind permission of Warner Bros. Entertainment, Inc., ©1938. The photographic reproductions of Korngold's short score, sketches, and cue sheets are courtesy of the Erich Wolfgang Korngold Collection, Music Division, Library of Congress, with the kind permission of Kathrin Korngold Hubbard. The extracts from Hugo Friedhofer's oral history are ©1974 American Film Institute, and the "Miß Austria" excerpt from *Rosen aus Florida* is ©1929 by Schott Musik International & Co. KG, Mainz, Germany. Reproduced by permission of Schott & Co. Limited, London.

Given that one of my aims in writing this book was to shatter the romantic myth of single authorship, it seems appropriate to acknowledge the many debts I owe to individuals, without whose help this book would not have been written, and whose voices speak throughout the text. Kathrin Korngold Hubbard's support has been invaluable, as have the efforts of Haden Guest, Randi Hokett, and Noelle Carter at Warner Bros. archives. I would also like to thank Danny Gould, Joseph Bille, Dave Olsen, Jack Rosner, and Jeremy N. Williams of Warner Bros.; Nicole Echle at Schott; Colin Green at Music Distribution Services Ltd.; and Catherine Rivers and Bonnie Coles at the Library of Congress. Brendan Carroll has been a constant source of clarification on all matters Korngoldian, and Rudy Behlmer and John Morgan have provided me with all sorts of useful *Robin Hood* information. Thanks also go to John Newton for taking the time to dig out his set of *Robin Hood* discs, to William H. Rosar for his help in tracking down Hugo Fried-hofer's oral history, and to Bill Wrobel for checking a number of items in the Warner Bros. archives on my behalf, and for his hospitality while I was in Los Angeles. Daniel Gallagher, James Longstaffe, and Nicho-las Attfield all read portions of the manuscript and/or listened to vari-ous ideas, and David Cooper's advice on a number of points was most helpful. I am particularly grateful to Prof. Peter Franklin for lending me copies of the films and for his unswerving enthusiasm for all things Korngoldian.

City University allowed me time to complete the book, for which I am thankful, and I would especially like to acknowledge the contribu-tion of my series editor, Kate Daubney. Her constant support and many useful suggestions have been invaluable.

INTRODUCTION

WHAT'S IN A TITLE?

The Adventures of Robin Hood (1938) is often lauded as one of the great film scores, one that helped define a style of film-scoring commonly referred to as 'classic.'[1] Its status is no doubt aided by the remarkable cultural cachet attached to its composer, Erich Wolfgang Korngold, a figure of increasing interest to musicology for his engagement with both high art and popular culture, and one of the most celebrated opera composers of his day.[2] When Korngold arrived in Hollywood in 1934 to work for Warner Bros. on Mendelssohn's music for their lavish version of *A Midsummer Night's Dream*, he did so at the invitation of Max Reinhardt, and not with the intention of forging a career in this newest of art forms. Nevertheless, in 1935 Korngold wrote his first original film score for *Captain Blood*, again for Warner Bros., and followed it with further scores, including *The Prince and the Pauper*, *Another Dawn*, and *Anthony Adverse*. Yet, in these early years of his film music career he still regarded himself as primarily a composer for the concert hall and opera house—even if his level of fame had peaked in the early 1920s—and periodically returned to Europe to continue composing 'high art' music. Political events intervened, however, and the Nazi annexation of his native Austria forced Korngold, as a Jew, into Hollywood exile; indeed, as will be seen in chapter 4, it would not be too glib to claim that *Robin Hood* saved his life.

By the time he came to score *The Adventures of Robin Hood* in 1938, Korngold was justifiably heralded in this newest area of musical composition. He followed the success of *Robin Hood*, which like *Anthony Adverse* before it won an Academy Award for its music, with scores to such Warner classics as *Juarez*, *The Private Lives of Elizabeth*

1

and Essex, The Sea Hawk, Kings Row, and *Deception*. Yet while Korngold's contributions to these film scores are beyond question, his renown as a high-art composer has somewhat overshadowed the importance of other figures integral to the sound of these film scores, and obscured the role played by the listener/viewer in creating their musical meanings.

The title of this volume, then, could be considered as something of a misnomer in that it implies a somewhat romanticized view of both the 'author' and the 'work.' It suggests that a unitary, identifiable author (Korngold) created a discrete aesthetic object (the score to *The Adventures of Robin Hood*) at a particular time (1938). Furthermore, it perhaps implies that this score has its own particular communicable meanings that are passively received by us, the listeners, and which require an explication of the composer's 'intentions' to effect an understanding of the musical 'work.' This romanticized attitude toward authorship is, in fact, rather common in film music literature that seeks to elevate the film score to the perceived status of 'high art' music, with its canons of composers and works.[3] Yet, recent trends in musicology have questioned those very canons and challenged composer-centered discourse and the primacy of the work-concept itself. We must surely wonder, then, whether the relatively youthful discipline of film musicology should repeat these traditional canon-forming practices or instead learn from recent changes in musicological thought and question the romantic aesthetic. As will become clear, the romanticized views of film score authorship and the 'musical work' implied by the title have the ability to restrict both a historical understanding of the way in which film scores were produced in the 1930s and 1940s, and the way in which these scores can be read: readings that are restricted by the notion of a composer's 'intentions' are limited indeed.

Rather than view this film score—or any of Korngold's film scores—as 'works' authored by a single musical persona, it seems more appropriate to consider them in the context (quite literally) of the post-structuralist idea of Text. First outlined by Barthes, Kristeva, Foucault, and others in the 1960s and 1970s, this notion conceived the novel, and thus by implication any other artistic production, not as a discrete aesthetic object, but as part of a network of meaning. The novel's meanings were not contained solely within the words of a particular book, but were intrinsically dependent on the existence of other writings: the new object of 'Text' could thus encompass numerous 'Works.' As Barthes put it:

> The Text is plural. Which is not simply to say that it has several meanings, but that it accomplishes the very plural of meaning...The Text is not a co-existence of meanings but a passage, an overcrossing; thus it answers not to an interpretation, even a liberal one, but to an explosion, a dissemination.[4]

Furthermore, this resulted in a new conception of the author that saw him/her as not the originator of meaning, but merely one voice in the tapestry-like weave of the Text. This 'death of the author,' as it was famously termed by Barthes, resulted in the 'birth of the reader' and a new emphasis on the reader's role in 'authoring' meaning. This post-structuralist approach to literature has, somewhat belatedly, been influential in musicological circles grappling with the thorny issue of musical meaning. As Michael Klein points out, once we start to ask what music means, we cease dealing with it as a Work and start our struggle with it as Text, and "as another text to be interpreted in the intertext around a work, the author has no transcendental power to close interpretation and fix meaning in place."[5]

What the present volume seeks to do, then, is to effect a transformation of our understanding of Korngold's score to *The Adventures of Robin Hood* from Work to Text; to show that the object of the film score is not 'hermetically sealed,' somehow unaffected by other film scores or musics, but part of a Text or Texts—a Korngoldian Text or a Film Music Text, for instance. The author figure is perhaps never more alive than when proclaimed dead, and Korngold as author, therefore, is never entirely absent—merely fragmented. As a result, there are numerous authorial voices present in a Korngold score: many of them are Korngold's own, though not all are contemporary with the film, and they may be mediated through the role of an orchestrator; some are created by the special productive circumstances of the studio system in which Korngold worked, allowing other figures an input into the music's content; while others, still, are the product of the reader's role in the process, identifying allusions to other composers or foregrounding some voices at the expense of others. It is the weave of these voices, though, that creates the Text of a film score, and ultimately the role of the reader/viewer/listener is potentially the most important element in controlling this weave and creating the score's meaning.

The score to *The Adventures of Robin Hood* will be revealed, then, as a very much more complicated object than the title of this volume might initially suggest. Chapter 1 concentrates on Korngold's engagement with the studio system, a production practice that had at its heart collaboration, and therefore the interplay between numerous authorial voices. Chapter 2 looks at Korngold's technique of film scoring and reveals the multiple voices of Korngold's musical persona to be a major facet of his compositional style, while chapter 3 examines the film's critical and historical contexts. Chapter 4 is an in-depth look at the processes involved in producing the score, revealing its complicated genesis and the different ways in which the score can be experienced—in short, its 'Text-like' characteristics. Finally, chapter 5 attempts to assess how the differing critical voices revealed in the preceding chapters are pulled together by the reader/viewer/listener to create the score's meaning. This weave of voices is mediated through the notion of convention, and the chapter will ask whether some of these readings are felt universally—thus making the musical effect part of a film music 'language' available for other composers to use—or whether each individual constructs his/her own different meaning. Since Korngold is perceived to have established a model for other film composers to follow, the answer to this question might prompt us to reconsider the role of convention in discussions of Korngold and in film music generally.

1

KORNGOLD
AND THE STUDIO SYSTEM

Erich Wolfgang Korngold's period of activity in Hollywood from 1934 to 1946 coincided with the high point of the studio system,[1] and it is within the context of this collaborative approach to cinema that his output must be placed. Though Korngold, as a celebrated European émigré, enjoyed a certain amount of creative freedom in comparison with other figures at Warner Bros., he was still required to tailor his working methods to those in place at the studio. He worked closely with staff orchestrators, and his music was, in all likelihood, subject to the opinions of executive producer Hal B. Wallis and, to a lesser extent perhaps, the music director, Leo F. Forbstein. This might suggest the image of a famous composer forced to compromise his artistic vision by the multiple authorial voices of an impersonal factory-like machine. Instead, Korngold himself should be seen as a complex mix of musical voices, rich with accrued associations from Viennese opera and operetta, engaged with a collaborative and largely supportive human system that enriched as much as it restricted.

The Studio System

The Hollywood studio system in place at the major movie corporations in the mid- to late 1930s was a regimented production arrangement that compartmentalized labor and ensured that quality films could be produced with the maximum level of efficiency. While the phrase "studio system" also describes the self-preserving oligarchy established by the vertically integrated studios[2] (Twentieth Century-Fox, Warner Bros.,

5

Paramount, MGM, and RKO) and their smaller partners (United Artists, Universal, and Columbia) in the mid-1920s, which lasted until the
early 1950s, what concerns us here are the common production practices in place at these studios. These practices extended across all areas
of movie production, including music.

While the studios had relied on a certain compartmentalization of
labor in separate production departments under the old central producers, the changes brought about in the early 1930s by the producer-unit
system represented a significant step forward in efficiency. The producer-unit system divided the production of films between teams of
dedicated units, each headed by a producer-supervisor and each responsible for a certain number of films per year. It was first proposed by
David O. Selznick as a means of restoring artistic creativity supposedly
lost under 'factory production,'[3] but it was the economic advantages
that likely won over studio executives struggling in the midst of the
Depression. Columbia Pictures adopted the system first in October
1931, and it soon spread to the other studios. Implicit in the producer-
unit system's division of labor was an accompanying demarcation of
genre: each unit could be organized to produce a certain type of film
and would accrue personnel accordingly, including contracted directors
and stars. At Warner Bros., for example, Executive in Charge of Production Hal B. Wallis had six supervisors working under him.[4] Of
these, Henry Blanke tended to work on the prestige pictures, often
biopics starring Paul Muni and directed by William Dieterle; Lou
Edelman handled service pictures and 'headliners,' contemporary stories lifted from the newspapers; and Brian Foy produced the studio's B-
pictures. As Janet Staiger has demonstrated, this division of labor was
reinforced by the activities of the unions and by the traditions of public
award ceremonies that rewarded contributions to strongly demarcated
fields.[5]

A factory or assembly-line analogy in connection with these production practices became common, no matter how complex the nature
of the personal creative relationships involved. Lewis Jacobs, for example, blamed the system, and its Wall Street backers, for a decline in
directorial power and an accompanying slump in creativity.[6] He saw
the vast capital required by the conversion to sound film in 1927 as the
underlying reason for this commercialization. In the 1950s, the *auteurist* critics of the Parisian journal *Cahiers du cinéma* seized upon
this view of the system, representing as it did an industrial hegemony
that stifled the creative activity of the individual. In their elevation of
Hollywood directors Howard Hawks, Douglas Sirk, and Alfred Hitch-

cock, critics required the studio system to be an impersonal machine-like entity that, entirely motivated by profit, restricted the creative activities of individuals. True *auteurs* would rise above these restrictions and stamp their individuality upon the films they made.

Auteur critics thus chose to ignore anything in the films they examined that, though entirely admirable, stemmed from a common fund of expression. While the picture of the system as a factory-like production machine seems to be an idealization,[7] more recent studies of the studio system have sought to stress the complexities of relations between various collaborators in the motion picture industry. In this regard, many have seized upon André Bazin's self-acknowledged distance from the more extreme views of some of his fellow contributors to *Cahiers du cinéma*:

> The American cinema is a classical art, but why not then admire in it what is most admirable, i.e. not only the talent of this or that film-maker, but the genius of the system, the richness of its ever-vigorous tradition, and its fertility when it comes into contact with new elements.[8]

Thomas Schatz, for example, quotes the above in the preface of his 1989 book, *The Genius of the System*. Schatz elevates a view of classical Hollywood cinema that brings to the fore the negotiation and struggle between various creative elements:

> [*Auteurism* effectively stalled] film history and criticism in a prolonged state of adolescent romanticism...But the closer we look at Hollywood's relations of power and hierarchy of authority during the studio era, at its division of labor and assembly-line production process, the less sense it makes to assess filmmaking or film style in terms of the individual director—or *any* individual, for that matter.[9]

The compartmentalization of labor represented by the studio system in the 1930s also extended to the production of music; the power relations and hierarchy of authority to which Schatz refers have as much relevance for the studio music departments as any other. The image of the studio system as the factory-like destroyer of musical creativity is, however, still firmly entrenched. One only has to mention the 'butchery' of scores by canonic composers such as Bernard Herrmann or Alfred Newman by their respective studios, to invoke this implicit understanding. Like the *auteur* theorists, this cliché can be used as a means of boosting the creative image of the individual at the expense of collaborative production practices. The portrayal of the composer's relationship with the institution of the Hollywood studio has rarely been questioned, much less aggressively interrogated—though Caryl Flinn, in arguing that this attitude can be traced back to nineteenth-century romanticism, is a notable exception.[10] The realities of the relationship suggest a similar level of collaborative negotiation and struggle to that found in other areas of production. As Flinn has pointed out, though, by attempting to appropriate the romantic myth of the single creative genius, film composers forfeited the protection offered by unions and other labor organizations.[11]

A studio music department would be responsible for all the musical requirements of a film, from hiring composers, orchestrators, and arrangers to gaining copyright permissions, choosing preexisting library music, and supervising the recording of any original score by a studio orchestra. During Korngold's early years working for Warner Bros., for example, the perceived importance of the music director was reflected in his status at award ceremonies: when the score for *Anthony Adverse* won the Academy Award for Best Musical Score on 4 March 1937, the recipient was announced as Leo F. Forbstein, the head of the music department; Korngold as 'composer' did not rate a mention. Though this practice was to change by the time the score for *The Adventures of Robin Hood* won in the same category, it is perhaps indicative of the power that the music directors wielded. Nor was this power necessarily a negative intrusion on the creative process. Though in Forbstein's case he was more an administrator than a musician, as staff orchestrator Hugo Friedhofer was to remark, "We were all cogs in [Forbstein's] well-oiled machine."[12]

The input of studio executives like Hal Wallis at Warner Bros. could also have a significant effect on the music used in a film. Wallis was particularly attuned to the power of music and would refer to it in his cutting notes. For Korngold's first original feature, *Captain Blood* (1935), Wallis wrote five single-spaced pages of instructional notes. Kathryn Kalinak reproduces a facsimile page in her book *Settling the Score*:

> Lose the music under the KNG JAMES sequence, where he sends the slaves to Jamaica, and bring the music up a little when it comes in now, just when KING JAMES speaks the last speech is where the music should start...Take the music out under the scene with BAYNES at his bedside, and start it up again when the guards come toward the place...Take out the one little piece of music between the girl and the boy when the girl is on horse-back, before FLYNN gets on to go and take care of the GOVERNOR...Lose the scoring in back

of the voices as...CAPTAIN BLOOD'S row boat pulls up along side...We just hear the singing until the men rush down stairs, then pick up that music.[13]

Though a producer's musical ability could vary drastically (Friedhofer noted with characteristic acerbic wit that their "musical tastes are, in a great many instances, dictated by the kind of phonograph records that their wives buy"),[14] one cannot doubt their proclivity for influencing the sound of a film score. Indeed, Max Steiner recognized this fact when commenting:

> A thousand and one things can happen to a music sound track from the time it leaves the composer's brain until it is heard by the audience. I have had pictures which did not require any music whatsoever, according to the producers. Some of these turned out to be 100 per cent underscoring jobs. On other pictures I was told that a certain film could not be released without an entire underscoring job, and I would work for weeks, day and night. When the finished product left the studio to go to the exchanges, only 60 per cent of all the music written remained.[15]

Similarly, Bernard Herrmann's horror at seeing his score for *The Magnificent Ambersons* replaced in part by the music of Roy Webb has been well documented,[16] and though it perpetuates the romantic notion of a work created before it is passed to the studio for commercial butchery, it shows that the composer was not regarded by the studio as a figure with authority over the finished product. Indeed, during the studio era, most composers relinquished their ownership rights to the studio.[17]

The smaller major studios such as Universal, Columbia, and United Artists, and the low-budget corporations like Republic or Monogram Pictures, would often choose a more economical approach to scoring than the larger majors like Warner Bros. or MGM. Universal reused original musical material in different movies or serials, sanctioned collaboration between multiple composers, and even used libraries of preexisting 'classics.' For its 1932 horror film *The Mummy*, for example, half of James Dietrich's score was replaced with stock melodies from the studio's library, including extracts from Tchaikovsky's *Swan Lake*.[18] Nor were such practices restricted to smaller studios, though they tended to use them to a greater degree. Portions of Steiner's 1933 score for *King Kong*, for example, turned up in later RKO features *Last of the Mohicans*, *We're Only Human*, and *The Last Days of Pompei*[19] and the score for *Gone with the Wind* includes mate-

rial composed by Hugo Friedhofer, Heinz Roemheld, and Adolph
Deutsch, in addition to the credited Max Steiner:

> And the pressure [of scoring to the deadline] was so great that Max
> [Steiner] finally decided that we'd better call in some other people to
> orchestrate. And he put me [Friedhofer] on the job of sort of super-
> vising over these guys, and writing some of the score, based on his
> material, of course...Maurice DePackh was one. Reginald Bassett
> was following me, on the stuff that I was writing. Heinz Roemheld
> did one or two sequences. I don't know who orchestrated for him.
> And Adolph Deutsch did one very striking sequence, the whole thing,
> the siege of Atlanta, with all the wounded lying around, and the fire
> and the whole bit. But the score was fundamentally—the material—
> was all Max's really...There's a very famous scene, one of the first
> really bloody scenes on the screen—the Yankee deserter, who gets
> shot by Scarlett. That was mine. And also the famous seduction
> scene, which started with Gable standing behind Scarlett...He ulti-
> mately picks her up and carries her upstairs, and fade out, fade in, to
> next morning, with Scarlett sitting up in bed, with this complacent,
> pussy-cat smile on her face. And there were some other, minor things
> that I did throughout.[20]

© 1974 American Film Institute

Even Korngold provided uncredited cues for *Hearts Divided* (1936)
and *The Green Pastures* (1936), and refused payment for the latter.[21]

Financial considerations were, of course, a motivation for these
practices, as David O. Selznick noted in 1947:

> I suggest that we make immediate investigations of the costs of the
> scores of other A pictures produced by the major studios and by the
> independents...I think also that we don't do nearly enough of using
> old music...For many years I have considered it absolute nonsense
> that the great music of the world, all available to us, was not used in
> pictures simply because of the ego and selfish interests of the com-
> posers whom we engaged...There are certain pictures which abso-
> lutely require original music, in whole or in part. There are others that
> don't require any original music, or certainly very little.[22]

David Raksin talks at length about the collaborative practices in play
during the studio era in his article "Holding a Nineteenth-Century Pedal
at Twentieth Century-Fox." Although he admits that "while the better
films were usually handed to a single composer, very often scores were
done by teams—even when there was no particular hurry. I myself

worked in this way at nearly every studio in town."[23] This 'team composition' is described by Raksin as a remarkably smooth process that involved few rivalries or creative disputes. When a new film was turned over to the music department, the staff would gather in the projection room to run the film and determine where music was required. When the layout for each reel was complete, timing sheets would be prepared, and the composers (Raksin, David Buttolph, and Cy Mockridge) would retire to their respective studios to compose the material they had assigned themselves. Upon reconvening with several versions of each theme, they would discuss which worked best and, when the timing sheets were ready, go away with each other's themes to compose the score.

Music departments also kept a staff of orchestrators on hand to aid composers, dividing the labor and thus making maximum use of the limited time available for a film's postproduction. While composers were certainly able, and would have preferred, to orchestrate their own music, the time pressures involved made delegation essential, albeit with copious instructions. Bernard Herrmann was one of the few composers afforded the luxury of orchestrating his own music. No matter how detailed these instructions were, though, the art of orchestration is undeniably a creative process that adds an extra layer of authorship to a film score. Ken Darby relates a conversation he had with Alfred Newman's orchestrators that reveals much about Newman's conception of their importance:

> Years before [the work on *The Greatest Story Ever Told* in 1964], Leo [Shuken] and Jack [Hayes] had called me aside to say, "This is crazy, man. Al's sketches are so complete, and annotated so precisely, that a *copyist* could lay them out on the score paper. What do you need orchestrators for?"
>
> I answered them a bit impatiently. "You dopes! A copyist would put it down exactly as it is. Both of you have seen the film. You know the substance of the scene and the intent of the composer. If either one of you has the faintest feeling in the seat of your pants that Poppy's [Newman's nickname] choice of instruments is in some subtle way wrong, or could be improved by the addition of another instrument—or placed in another octave—and *don't follow that hunch*, then you're making no contribution at all, and sooner than later he'll catch up on it and raise hell. That's why he loves you guys. You're great orchestrators, *not* copyists. So—go orchestrate![24]

The relationship between a composer and his orchestrator(s) could be an intensely positive creative collaboration. Hugo Friedhofer, the trust-

ed orchestrator of both Korngold and Max Steiner, and later a film
composer in his own right, tells a story in his oral history about his contributions to Steiner's *Casablanca* score:

> I know that [Steiner] didn't have the feeling that the thing ["As Time
> Goes By"] would work in the orchestra at all, because he had a con-
> cept of it as being kind of a square tune, which requires translation
> from what's in the printed piano part to a more relaxed version. You
> know, you can't play (SINGING) "Ta-ta, ta-ta, ta-*ta* Ta-ta, ta-ta, ta-
> *ta*," which is what it is, in the original. So, I say this with all modesty,
> I said, "Max, think of it this way, (AGAIN SINGING "AS TIME
> GOES BY," BUT VERY BROADLY) "Dah-dum-bah, duh, duh,
> *duhm*. Bah-dim-bah, dah, dah, *dahm*," with triplet phrasing. He kind
> of thought about it, and that's the way it came out.[25]

Clearly an orchestrator's role in film score production could be significant on a creative level.

While the above discussion of a music department's collaborative
practices may seem far removed from the 'art' music traditions with
which Korngold was familiar, much recent musicological research has
stressed the collaboration found in the opera house and ballet theater.
Roger Parker has explored the idea of opera as a multiple-authored text
with competing and destabilizing authorial intentions between the personas of composer, librettist, impresario, set designers, *regisseurs*, and
principal singers;[26] and John McGinness's discussion of Debussy's
Jeux argues that the ballet's conception was an unashamed collaboration between Debussy, Diaghilev, and Nijinsky.[27] Similarly, Tchaikovsky's collaborations with balletmasters, and the contractual authority of the latter over the former, also provide interesting parallels to the
Hollywood studio system.[28] Korngold himself, in his involvement with
operetta adaptations, sometimes worked with orchestrators Franz Ko-
priva, Julius Bittner, and Bruno Granichstaedten, and his choice of music in these operettas was frequently dictated by the need for a 'Tauber-
lied' to showcase the talents of legendary tenor Richard Tauber.[29] The
idea of Korngold working within a collaborative music department was
not so great a step, and though he was to gain substantially more power
as a composer than was common, he would always remain subject to
the needs of the film and, ultimately, the opinions of Hal Wallis.

Korngold's first encounter with the studio system came in 1934
when he was lured to Hollywood by his old friend and operetta collabo-
rator, the impresario Max Reinhardt. Reinhardt, having been forced out

of German theatrical life by the Nazis, had left for America, and, working on a film adaptation of his Hollywood Bowl production of *A Midsummer Night's Dream*, begged Korngold to come to Los Angeles to work with him. The cable mentioned only six or eight weeks of work and the intrigued Korngold could not help but agree to the persuasive Reinhardt, though his domineering father, Julius, was opposed to the trip. Korngold arrived in America with his wife, Luzi, on 30 October 1934, and once they were settled in Los Angeles, the composer paid a visit to the Warner Bros. studios in Burbank. Producer Henry Blanke introduced him to Jack Warner and Leo Forbstein and took him on a tour of the sound stage, where a recording was taking place. Korngold then famously asked, "How long does a foot of film last in music?" a question that supposedly no one had considered before. Upon finding out the answer (two-thirds of a second), the composer commented that this was exactly equal to the first two bars of the Mendelssohn *Midsummer Night's Dream* Scherzo.[30]

Korngold's involvement with the project differed greatly from future film scores and in many ways represented only a partial engagement with the studio system's creative processes. He was responsible for arranging the Mendelssohn music, choosing to augment the incidental music to *A Midsummer Night's Dream* with extracts from the Scottish Symphony (No. 3) and several of the *Lieder ohne Worte*, and composing a number of short linking passages in the style of the nineteenth-century composer. Korngold's ability to allow another composer's musical voice to speak through his own Viennese orchestral idiom is striking, though, and entirely in keeping with the studio system's collaborative practices. Unlike *The Adventures of Robin Hood*, however, where Korngold became involved only after filming was completed, *A Midsummer Night's Dream*, with its ballet sequences and sung passages, required the composer to be on set during filming. He commented upon this unusual arrangement in an article written in 1940:

> I had to make preliminary recordings, the so-called playbacks, of Mendelssohn's scherzo and nocturne, which were relayed over huge loudspeakers during the actual filming. Further, I conducted the orchestra on stage for complicated, simultaneous "takes", and lastly, after the film was cut, I conducted a number of music pieces which were inserted in the completed picture as background music. In addition, however, I had to invent another, *new* method which was a combination of all three techniques and which was for music accompanying the *spoken word*. I wrote out the music in advance, conducted—without orchestra—the actor on the stage in order to make

him speak his lines in the required rhythm, and then, sometimes
weeks later, guided by earphones, I recorded the orchestral part.[31]

The level of involvement with the production enjoyed by Korngold was
perhaps close to that of earlier collaborations with Reinhardt in Europe,
and it evidently irked Hal Wallis. In a memo of December 1934, Wallis
writes:

> I am concerned about the fact that Korngold is stepping in too much
> as to how people should speak and how it is going to fit in with his
> music, and I would rather not have him on the set at all if this is go-
> ing to be the case.[32]

Korngold remained on set and the production, which had gone vastly
over budget and was dreadfully behind schedule, finally finished shooting on 26 February 1935. Korngold stayed until 30 April working on
the film's postproduction before heading home for Vienna to continue
work on his fifth opera, *Die Kathrin*. Despite the poor commercial performance of *A Midsummer Night's Dream* (at over $1.5 million it was
the most expensive Warner Bros. film to date and barely made back its
money), the film announced the arrival of Warner Bros. into the prestige film market; and the studio was therefore keen to acquire Korngold's services on a more permanent basis.

Korngold was soon invited back to Hollywood by Paramount to
work with director Ernst Lubitsch and singer Jan Kiepura (who had
appeared in Korngold's fourth opera, *Das Wunder der Heliane*) on its
musical *Give Us This Night*. By this time, the Nazis had banned Korngold's works in Germany, and he could no longer rely on a regular in-
come from royalties. The lucrative offer thus proved, once again, too
tempting to refuse, and the Korngolds, this time accompanied by their
sons Georg and Ernst, headed back to California. While working on
Give Us This Night, however, Korngold was asked to score Warner's
new swashbuckling spectacular, *Captain Blood*, starring the unknown
pairing of Errol Flynn and Olivia de Havilland. It was to start Korngold
on the road that would lead to *The Adventures of Robin Hood* barely
three years later.

Despite Wallis's concerns, Korngold's early encounters with the
music department at Warner Bros. should not be seen as the forced
confrontation between an individual and the monolithic bureaucracy of
'the system.' While the system itself was human and predicated on
creative collaboration, Korngold's musical persona was also a rich tapestry of musical voices gained from his musical upbringing and early

career in *fin-de-siècle* Vienna. His scores thus carry around with them the often sublimated, but sometimes openly celebrated, musical voices of Mahler, Richard Strauss, and Zemlinsky, in addition to the 'lighter' traditions of Johann Strauss II and Leo Fall and the French modernism of Dukas.

Korngold's Viennese Background

With regards to modern German music, my biggest hope lies with Erich Wolfgang Korngold...he has so much talent that he could give half of it away and still have enough left for himself.

In this oft-quoted 1921 assessment of Korngold, Giacomo Puccini appears to encapsulate the combination of admiration and jealousy that surrounded the young composer in Vienna—admiration because the man was so obviously "a genius" and was so proclaimed by Gustav Mahler and Richard Strauss;[33] jealousy because many suspected his success was due in no small part to the promoting activities of Erich's powerful father, Dr. Julius Korngold, chief music critic at the *Neue Freie Presse*. Indeed, negative reactions to the Korngolds were also potentially motivated by the anti-Semitism that was rife in Austria's capital throughout the early twentieth century. Puccini himself, however, was firmly in the former camp: he was a true friend and, along with Richard Strauss, an admirer of Korngold.

Erich Wolfgang Korngold was born on 29 May 1897 in the Moravian capital Brün (now Brno in the Czech Republic) to a family that, although Jewish, saw themselves as primarily Austrian. His middle name, chosen by his father in homage to Mozart, proved strangely prophetic, because the young Erich proved himself as great a child prodigy as his illustrious namesake. It is clear, however, that Julius's influence on Erich's life extended far beyond choosing an apposite name. Having studied harmony with Anton Bruckner and formed alliances with Johannes Brahms and the critic Eduard Hanslick, Julius was destined for great things himself. In November 1901 he and his young family moved to Vienna, the musical capital of the world, where he became Hanslick's assistant at the *Neue Freie Presse*. Just three years later, upon Hanslick's death, Julius became the most powerful music critic in Vienna, and with his son already displaying signs of prodigious musical talent, as both a pianist and composer, he was in the perfect position to help (and often inadvertently hinder) Erich's career. Julius, however, was anxious not to reveal his son's talent too early and took care to shield Erich from premature public exposure, trusting his musical education to Alexander von Zemlinsky.

Vienna at this time was at the vanguard of musical modernism with Mahler's tenure at the Hofoper (the Imperial Opera House) from 1897 to 1907 having introduced new works by Puccini, Pfitzner, and Richard Strauss. Zemlinsky and his circle—including Arnold Schoenberg, Alban Berg, and Anton von Webern—idolized Mahler, and when he left the Hofoper for opportunities in New York, they continued his pioneering policies. Mahler had been the honorary president of Zemlinsky's own *Vereinigung schaffender Tonkünstler*, which had given the first performances of Schoenberg's *Pelleas und Melisande* and Bartók's First Orchestral Suite in 1905, and it was Zemlinsky who conducted the Viennese premiere of Dukas's modernist opera *Ariane et Barbe-bleu* in 1908, a work that was to have a profound effect on the young Korngold.

Viennese society's introduction to the young prodigy finally took place on 14 April 1910 with the first public performance of Korngold's ballet pantomime *Der Schneemann* (The Snowman). This first foray into the world of drama set the young composer on the road toward the operatic triumphs of the next twenty years, and its première, attended by the upper echelons of Austrian aristocracy, was soon the talk of Vienna. Though the orchestral version of *Der Schneemann* was orchestrated by Zemlinsky, Korngold soon displayed a facility in this regard equal to his compositional gifts, composing and orchestrating the *Schauspiel Ouvertüre* of 1911 and following it with the Sinfonietta of 1912. The latter included a motto theme based on a series of interlocked rising fourths that Korngold named the *Motiv des Fröhlichen Herzens* (the motif of the cheerful heart) and which became a musical signature that appeared in works throughout his career. Further premières followed to public and critical acclaim, though rumblings against Julius's aggressive support for his son's music at the expenses of others' continued. Erich's talent was such, though, that even the negative press surrounding his father couldn't diminish Vienna's enthusiasm for his music, an enthusiasm that rapidly spread throughout the Western world. His works were conducted by such eminent figures as Felix Weingartner, Arthur Nikisch, and Sir Henry Wood—remarkable when one considers that the young Korngold was still a teenager.

By 1913, the tension inherent in Viennese music between a progressive modernism and the reactionary character of traditional Viennese folk-inspired music had become more apparent: in March, a concert conducted by Schoenberg that featured music by himself, Berg, Webern, Zemlinsky, and the now deceased Mahler prompted a riot that required police intervention. Similarly the rising religious tensions that had seen the founding of a rapidly growing *Verein zur Abwehr des Antisemitismus* (Society for the Defense Against Anti-Semitism) in 1891, intersected with the artistic debate: the modernism of Schoenberg, Wellesz, and Eduard Steuermann was firmly allied with Judaism, while the defenders of Viennese tradition, such as Joseph Marx and Franz Schmidt, were Catholic. Korngold, with his controversial father (who broadly sided with the conservative factions) was thrust into this hotbed of religious and aesthetic tension.

In the same year as Schoenberg's infamous concert, Korngold embarked on his operatic career, from which his natural affinity with the film score's dramatic requirements undoubtedly grew. In 1913 he began the composition of a one-act *opera buffa* entitled *Der Ring des Polykrates* based on a drama by Heinrich Teweles. A lighthearted domestic tale of love, jealousy, and misunderstanding, *Polykrates*—like later dramatic scenarios found in both Korngold's operas and film scores—features a musician as the main protagonist. Wilhelm Arndt is the newly appointed court music director whose great luck in his professional and personal life is threatened by his jealous friend Peter Vogel, who tries to disturb his wedded bliss. The setting, a small royal residence in Saxony in 1797, and the profession of Wilhelm and his music copyist, Florian, allow for some delightful references to Vienna's musical past. When Florian remembers being a copyist for "Mr. von Haydn" in Vienna and playing timpani in his symphonies, Korngold cheekily quotes the Andante from Haydn's "Surprise" Symphony No. 94.[34] Already, it seems, Korngold had recognized the importance of his musical heritage and allowed a musical voice from the past to speak through his music. It was this willingness to act as a conduit through which other voices, including his own past voices, could speak that perhaps allowed him to slot so neatly into the collaborative realities of the Hollywood studio system.

Polykrates was followed by a one-act companion piece, *Violanta*, which shared the program when it received its premiere on 28 March 1916 under the baton of a youthful Bruno Walter. Where *Polykrates* was comic, though, *Violanta* was tragic; and where *Polykrates* was scored for chamber orchestra, *Violanta* utilized a large orchestra with triple woodwind. Most notable, however, is the intense atmosphere and emotional maturity in evidence, as Korngold sets the tale of a fifteenth-

century noblewoman who vows to avenge the death of her sister only to
fall in love with the man who seduced her sister and caused her demise.

If *Der Ring des Polykrates* and *Violanta* marked Korngold as a
major operatic talent, though, his next opera cemented his global repu-
tation. *Die tote Stadt* (The Dead City)—based on the Georges Roden-
bach novel *Bruges la Morte*—received a double première in Hamburg
and Cologne on 4 December 1920. A full three-act opera with large
orchestra, it became one of the most successful in the repertoire; its
most memorable extract, Marietta's Lute Song "Glück, das mir
verblieb" was one of the most oft-sung and recorded soprano arias. As
with *Polykrates* before it, Korngold again allows another composer's
musical voice to speak through his own: Marietta and her friends are
performing *Robert le diable*, prompting a musical quotation of Meyer-
beer's opera at figure 187. These early operas, particularly *Violanta* and
Die tote Stadt, showcase Korngold's gifts for melody and chromatically
complex harmony and demonstrate his ease with sensational melodra-
matic plots.

Seven years elapsed before Korngold's next opera, *Das Wunder
der Heliane* (The Miracle of Heliane), appeared; yet at the time of its
première on 7 October 1927, *Heliane* was dragged into a debate about
the future of music, in which it was pitted against Ernst Krenek's *Jonny
spielt auf*. This, perhaps, is the start of the public rift between Korngold
and the modernism to which he'd previously felt some allegiance.
Julius Korngold, as one might expect, led the attack against Krenek's
work—which had also prompted protests from the growing Nazi
movement—and the Berlin press responded in kind, labeling *Heliane*
backward and conservative. By this time, Berlin had supplanted Vienna
as the leading center of musical modernism, with both Schoenberg and
Franz Schreker abandoning the Austrian capital in the 1920s. Nevertheless, the Viennese production of *Heliane* was broadcast live on radio
and its music received favorable reviews; it went on to enjoy success
throughout Europe, if not at the level afforded *Die tote Stadt*.

In 1923, already engaged with composing *Heliane*, Korngold had
begun another long-standing association with Viennese theatrical traditions by adapting and conducting a new performance of Johann Strauss
II's *Eine Nacht in Venedig*, featuring Richard Tauber. Not only did this
lucrative commission enable Korngold to marry Luise (Luzi) von Son-
nenthal, a union opposed by both sets of parents, but it also led to a
number of other operetta adaptations, including works by Offenbach
and, of particular interest to this study, Leo Fall. Korngold's work with
operetta adaptations also brought him into closer contact with Max

Reinhardt, whom he had known since his youth. At Christmas 1930, Reinhardt asked him to prepare Offenbach's score of *La Belle Hélène* for a new production, *Die schöne Helena*, in Berlin. Though the score was finished, unlike Fall's *Rosen aus Florida* on which he had worked in 1928, Korngold interpolated other pieces by Offenbach for some of the new scenes and, for others, composed new music himself. Operetta thus provided yet more encounters with musical voices from the past and enriched the cultural baggage that Korngold would take with him across the Atlantic. The discipline of working to a tight schedule would also serve him well during his years in Hollywood.

By this time, Korngold had also received his first invitations to work in film—not from America, but from the German studio UFA. Korngold turned down two opportunities to score movies due to operetta commitments[35] and continued his search for a new opera libretto, eventually finding it in Heinrich Eduard Jacob's novella *Die Magd von Aachen* (*The Maid of Aachen*), which became his fifth and last opera, *Die Kathrin*. The plot tells of the love of a Swiss servant girl (Kathrin) for a French soldier—who also happens to be a musician—their separation, and eventual reunion after many years. The original scenario called for the action to take place in World War I, and for the character of Kathrin to be German, thus resulting in a symbolic unification between the two nations; however, Hitler's rise to power ensured that Schott, Korngold's publisher, could not allow such a scenario, and it was Luzi who suggested that the opera be stripped of all political overtones and reset in 1930, allowing work to proceed.

When Reinhardt's offer turned up in 1934, Austria was a semifascist state with both anti-Semitism and anti-modernism on the increase. While Korngold was not the most prescient of political forecasters, he nevertheless agreed to Reinhardt's suggestion—despite having commenced work on *Die Kathrin*—and embarked on what he undoubtedly saw as a career sideshow, taking the musical language of Vienna with him. Although he would return to Vienna on a regular basis until 1938 and would return briefly after the war in an attempt to revive his European career, Korngold's fortunes were now firmly tied to the overtly collaborative practices of Hollywood.

2

KORNGOLD'S TECHNIQUE OF SCORING FILMS

Korngold's working methods on *A Midsummer Night's Dream* differed markedly in many respects from other films he worked on later at Warner Bros., including *The Adventures of Robin Hood*. This was a result of the unusual nature of the task, and his early involvement with the production process. Yet, the techniques he developed in 1934 were to serve him well throughout his film score career. Combined with his extensive experience in the world of opera and operetta, his innate approach to dramatic musical composition, and the ability to work with creative collaborators in the music department, they furnished Korngold with many of the skills he would require to produce film scores that were held in high regard by both the industry and the public.

The following discussion will therefore examine Korngold's normal working methods as a film composer—methods that are themselves shrouded in a certain amount of myth—before addressing particular features of his compositional style that are evidenced in the film scores, namely: Korngold's sensitivity to dialogue; his musical language; his commitment to, and use of, thematic structures; his demarcation of narrative space, including his sensitivity to scoring historical subjects; and his use of, and interaction with, diegetic music. Finally, Korngold's self-borrowings, perhaps the most intriguing facet of his compositional style, will be addressed in the broad context of theories of intertextuality.

The notion that music is somehow 'added on' to a preexisting narrative may be supported by the normal working methods of the Hollywood studio system; however, as spectators, we arguably perceive the narrative as an integrated structure, and to analyze the effect that music

21

has on narrative is, to some degree, a misrepresentation of how film works. As Michel Chion argues, "there is no soundtrack," that is, we cannot separate the individual film components and assess their impact on an overall structure of which they are an intrinsic part.[1] Throughout the following discussion—which necessarily concentrates on the techniques employed in Korngold's music—it must be remembered, therefore, that these scores are best appreciated as an integral part of the film.

Normal Working Methods

After *A Midsummer Night's Dream*, Korngold's involvement with the other films he worked on—with the exception of *Deception* and *Magic Fire*—was, in common with other studios and composers, mainly at the postproduction stage. While any diegetic music, such as the song sung by Olivia de Havilland in *The Private Lives of Elizabeth and Essex*, may have been prepared as 'prescoring' before shooting,[2] the underscoring would have waited until a rough edit was complete. Korngold is famous for his 'unusual' working methods, in that he is said to have composed on an upright piano in a projection room while the film was run in front of him. He noted in 1940, "I am not composing at a desk writing music mechanically, so to speak, for the lengths of film measured out by an assistant and accompanied with sketchy notes on the action...but I do my composing in the projection room."[3] Hugo Friedhofer also commented in his oral history for the American Film Institute that

> Korngold did all his work in the projection room—just improvised to the film. After seeing the film the first time, without fooling around at all, he would go home and start inventing themes. Then his next running would be in the projection room, with a small upright piano, and improvising on the material that he had dreamt up, to the film as it was run. He'd start making very rough sketches, which he'd then take home and refine. Then he'd come back the next day and check and double-check for timing and what-not. Never any marks on the film until he was about ready to record.[4]

© 1974 American Film Institute

This is implicitly painted in opposition to the kind of 'hacks' employed at other studios who, it might be assumed, didn't even watch the film, or at least watched it only once and composed away from the projection room in collaboration with their colleagues (as in David Raksin's experiences). Similarly, Friedhofer contrasts Korngold's methods with those of Max Steiner who, "after running the picture once, at the most twice, would depend entirely on the cue sheets which were supplied to him by his music editor."[5]

Korngold himself did acknowledge, though, that he sketched most of his initial themes away from the projection room;[6] famously, the regal theme he wrote for *Kings Row*, assuming it to be another story of kings and queens rather than the tale of small-town intrigue it actually is, was preserved when he came to read the script.[7] The idea that superior film music requires constant reference to the image does not necessarily stand up to scrutiny and perhaps merely betrays an ideological bias in favor of single creative figures working in isolation, the genius composer cocooned in his projection room.

Similarly, many have claimed that Korngold's renowned sense of timing did not necessitate any mechanical aid or the use of cue sheets (written descriptions of scenes with very precise timings indicating the length of on-screen events) to help him compose or record his music. Indeed both Korngold's and Friedhofer's comments at least suggest this: "[Korngold] had a built-in sense of the speed at which something should move. Steiner, on the other hand, always worked...to cue sheets, and also utilized the click track a great deal for tempos."[8] Korngold himself commented that "if the picture inspires me, I don't even have to count the seconds or feet."[9]

While Korngold's musical gifts are surely beyond question, this rather romanticized version of film score composition seems at odds with the evidence presented by the manuscript sources themselves. In the case of *The Adventures of Robin Hood*—evidently a film that did not inspire the composer—Korngold certainly made use of cue sheets (see chapter 4). In addition, while Korngold may not have used the Newman system of click tracks, flutter punches, and other mechanical aids when conducting his music, he seems to have marked his full score unusually precisely. At times—particularly before a change of time signature—a series of lines marks every beat, giving an indication of the required gesture.

Korngold's lofty position at Warner Bros., allowing him to pick and choose his assignments,[10] was certainly unusual, but there is little evidence, in *Robin Hood* at least, of the tremendous power ascribed to him by his orchestrator Hugo Friedhofer:

I can recall many instances when Korngold would go to the producer and say, "Look, can you give me a little more footage at the end of" whatever scene it was. "I feel that as the end of an act. I feel that there's a first act curtain there." And he would always get his way.[11]

© 1974 American Film Institute

Indeed, quite the contrary is the case. There are cuts made in cue 2B of the film that make little musical sense (see example 2.1) and would surely have been resisted by Korngold.

That the film contains such moments should perhaps encourage us to treat these claims with skepticism. Even Korngold's own comments reveal the authorial presence of men like Leo Forbstein and Hal Wallis:

It is entirely up to me to decide where in the picture to put music. But I always consult thoroughly with the music-chief whose judgment, based on years of experience, I consider highly important. I also keep the producer well informed and always secure his consent for my musical intentions first.[12]

And indeed, Friedhofer concedes that, in terms of where Korngold and Steiner placed music, "they always sat with the producer."[13]

Of course, Korngold did not work in isolation. He enjoyed a very close relationship with his orchestrators, Friedhofer in particular, and sometimes turned to them to compose cues. In *Captain Blood*, for example, several cues ("Street Scene" and "Spanish Soldier") were written by Milan Roder. Roder also composed the radio commercial heard in *Deception*, while the jazz arrangement of the Mendelssohn wedding march heard at Hollenius and Christine's wedding reception in the same film was prepared by Ray Heindorf. In the short score of *The Adventures of Robin Hood*, several parts of cues exist only in the hand of secondary orchestrator Roder. This suggests that Roder was involved in the production process of the score at an earlier stage than is commonly accepted. At the end of cue 10C, for example, Korngold writes "Segue Roder," and at the end of cue 1D, "Segue Roder Sortie." This "sortie" music refers to the opening passage of cue 1D; though there is a page of sketches for this music in Korngold's hand bound with the rest of the score, the only assembled version of the cue appears in Roder's handwriting. Similarly, Roder prepared the trailer music for the film, based on the existing cues but also providing a few bars of new material. Finally, the revisions made to the score after the film sneak-previewed (discussed in chapter 4) are not to be found in Korngold's hand in any of the sources. While this does not prove that they were written by the orchestrators, it at least suggests the possibility.

Example 2.1. Cuts to Cue 2B in *The Adventures of Robin Hood* **(Cut Bars Bracketed)**

Relationship with Orchestrators

Korngold's normal working relationship with his principal orchestrator, Hugo Friedhofer, was evidently a happy and mutually supportive one. Friedhofer's oral history gives us valuable insight into the dynamics of this partnership:

Well it was a very, very close association [working on *Captain Blood*]. He always liked to look at the scores. We'd discuss the sketches very thoroughly. He had a fantastic way of playing the piano with an orchestral style, so you could almost sense what he was hearing in the orchestra. He did not make an orchestral sketch, in four of five lines, as some do, and as I do personally, He wrote a piano part, actually. And sometimes there was a large hole in the middle, you know. It would be what lay conveniently under the right hand. You had to sort of be possessed of a certain clairvoyance, a kind of a musical crystal ball, to figure out whether that was the way he really wanted it, because sometimes he *did* want that wide open space in the middle. And sometimes the whole set-up, in the piano part, would have to be a certain extent re-voiced, or else filled out.

But the first few, he gave me half a dozen of his sketches, we discussed them, and then I took them home and orchestrated them. He seemed very pleased, and he made an extraordinary remark. He said, "You must be very well acquainted with the music of Gustav Mahler."[14]

© 1974 American Film Institute

Friedhofer further elaborated on these discussions, and he hints at the growing responsibility he assumed as their working relationship progressed in a 1967 letter to Rudy Behlmer:

We would sit together at the piano with the sequence to be orchestrated and he would play it through, with me filling in the occasional notes that were outside the capacities of ten fingers...After the run-through at the keyboard, there would be a detailed discussion of color in the orchestra. This was a give and take affair, with me telling him what I heard and he giving me his conception for what the color should be. Then I would make careful enquiry as to those places in his sketch which were capable of being set as they stood, i.e. without any re-voicing, changes of register, octave doubling, etc.

When I had completed the sections he had given me, he and I would go through the full score together and in detail. As time went on, he came to rely more and more on my discretion in the matter of color and voicing, and in many instances would discuss with me the orchestrations of sections which were to be farmed out to other orchestrators.[15]

Korngold's increasing trust meant that, in the case of *The Sea Wolf* (1941), Friedhofer was given carte blanche for the score's orchestration:

That was a very fine picture, and a little different than anything else that Korngold did over there [at Warner Bros.]. As a matter of fact, it was the picture on which he did me the honor of saying, "Look, you know a great deal more about how to orchestrate this kind of music," because it was very edgy, quite dissonant for the time. So he said, "I'm not going to tell you a thing about what to do with it." So he left it entirely up to me...I think that the only thing that we really discussed in enormous detail was a scene right at the beginning of the picture where this fog-bound San Francisco Bay is shown...because he had a beautiful texture laid out...with a million notes in it, but fun to do, nevertheless.[16]

© 1974 American Film Institute

Korngold's specific working methods on *The Adventures of Robin Hood* are discussed in detail in chapter 4.

Sensitivity to Dialogue

Korngold is frequently lauded for his sensitive response to scoring dialogue in films, leading to some wild claims that Korngold's awareness of the pitch of the actors' voices caused him to adjust the tonality of his music accordingly.[17] These rather spurious claims are probably derived from comments made by the director of *Anthony Adverse*, Mervyn LeRoy: "[Korngold] told me that he was always careful to take note of what pitch or register the actors were speaking in, and then he would score carefully so as not to interfere with it."[18] Tony Thomas, taking note of these comments perhaps, argued that while scoring *Anthony Adverse*, Korngold "came upon a technique that was later adapted by other composers—pitching the music just under the pitch of the voices and surging into pauses in the dialogue."[19] Similarly, Brendan Carroll has noted the way in which Korngold scored the scene in *Juarez* where Carlota kneels before the statue of the Madonna and the underscore seems to follow the rhythm of her speech pattern.[20] Violinist George Berris of the Warner Bros. orchestra also recalled Korngold telling the musicians that a theme in *Anthony Adverse* was written specifically with a line of dialogue in mind ("No Father, No Mother, No Name").[21] In the case of Korngold's work on *A Midsummer Night's Dream*, with its poetic language, such practices must have been the norm, as his comments about 'conducting' the actors reveal; however, in his other film scores, moments of recitation in this fashion are rare, and the idea that Korngold adjusted the *key* of the music to fit in with a kind of spoken recitation seems far more difficult to support. Characters rarely speak in monologue, and a scene in which two or more characters were speaking would logically require a bitonal or polytonal approach. Such approaches to tonality are rarely found in Korngold's film scores.

What these comments do reveal, however, is a highly attuned ear and a willingness to work as part of an overall sound design (a term not coined until Walter Murch's work several decades later). It is certainly the case that Korngold was acutely aware of dialogue, and the need to allow it space within the sound mix. At certain points in complex action cues, such as the duels in *The Adventures of Robin Hood* and *The Prince and the Pauper* or the opening sea battle in *The Sea Hawk*, the music will reach 'plateau notes,' or sustained chords, allowing the dialogue to be clearly heard without any complex musical accompaniment diverting the ear—the very relationship between dialogue and music that Thomas talks about. In *The Adventures of Robin Hood*, Korngold also made special notes on the cue sheets and in the short score where dialogue occurred. This sensitivity to the demands of dialogue was evidently part of his theatrical background: *Die Kathrin*, for example, contains scenes of extended dialogue and spoken recitation. These Korngold treats in a similar manner to the film scores, sometimes coordinating the accompaniment with the rhythm of the words (as at figure 45), at other times incorporating pauses into the music over which the dialogue can be spoken (two before figure 36).

This sensitivity to dialogue is not confined to Korngold, however, and was a major feature of Max Steiner's film scoring style. His unpublished autobiography *Notes to You* reveals a preoccupation with avoiding the pitch of the actors' voices: if the voice was low, for example, Steiner would write music in a high register, and vice versa.[22]

Musical Language

Korngold's musical language in his film scores does not differ hugely from his concert works and operas, though as his composition for the concert hall and opera house ceased for the duration of the war after his permanent move to Hollywood in 1938, it is difficult to assess how he might have varied the musical languages used. Korngold, himself, famously denied distinguishing at all, arguing, "Never have I differentiated between my music for the films and that for the operas and concert pieces."[23] An understanding of the musical language of the operas is therefore useful for our appreciation of the film scores.

In the case of Korngold's second opera, *Violanta*, the charged eroticism of the drama is matched by the intensity of the chromatic harmonic language and an economy of scale that perhaps foreshadowed the smaller forms available to him in film score composition. Indeed, Korngold's next opera, *Die tote Stadt*, despite its richly orchestrated textures, nevertheless sometimes sounds almost plain after the chromatic intensity of *Violanta*. Korngold's predilection for augmented triads—as heard in *Between Two Worlds*'s 'glass-breaking chord,' signaling the mortal world intruding on the afterlife—can also be traced to the altered ninth chord that opened *Violanta*.[24]

Das Wunder der Heliane (The Miracle of Heliane), a tale of love and resurrection infused with the passion of the early years of his marriage to Luzi, takes the Korngoldian harmonic language of *Violanta* to the extremes of chromaticism; at several points there are bichords that almost suggest bitonality. The opening chords of the resurrection theme which opens the opera, for example, consist of an F-sharp major triad, followed by superimposed A major and D major triads, and the offstage fanfares in the first scene of Act 3 consist of three overlapping tone pairs (F#-G#, B-C#, G-A). Korngold acknowledged in an interview with the *Neues Wiener Tagblatt* that the opera was harmonically more radical than either *Violanta* or *Die tote Stadt* and specifically referred to what he saw as the harmonic 'enrichments' of Schoenberg.[25] He also maintained, however, his continued allegiance to 'old music' and eschewed any dogmatic commitment to any one view, citing the 'inspired idea' as his only doctrine. Indeed the *Vier kleine Karikaturen für Kinder* of 1926, which parody the four leading modernists of the day (Schoenberg, Stravinsky, Bartók, and Hindemith), perhaps reveal something of Korngold's ambivalent attitude toward modernism. Certainly the modernist harmonic language of the piano concerto, the *Vier kleine karikaturan für Kinder*, and some parts of *Das Wunder der Heliane* is not the staple of the Korngold film score; however, he does not shy away from the use of modernism altogether, as the knife fight in *The Adventures of Robin Hood*, many moments in *The Sea Wolf*, or the dream sequences in *Devotion* attest. Indeed, Peter Franklin calls the scores of *Kings Row*, *Deception*, and *Between Two Worlds* "almost expressionistic."[26] Korngold's fondness for delayed harmonic resolution, seen throughout the operas (see the Act 2 *Vorspiel* from *Die tote Stadt*, for example), is likewise displayed throughout the film scores (see example 2.2).

Example 2.2. Delayed Resolution in Cue 5E of *The Adventures of Robin Hood*

Die Kathrin is subtitled "a folk opera"; as a result, its musical language is far more diatonic, in the first act at least, than the intense chromaticism of *Heliane*. It is thus closer to the musical language that Korngold employed in many of the film scores, particularly *Robin Hood*. Perhaps smarting from the unfavorable comparison of *Heliane* with *Jonny spielt auf*, *Die Kathrin* makes use of popular styles: Kathrin's aria "Ich soll dich nicht mehr wiedersehn," which bears a striking resemblance to "Glück, das mir verblieb," is described as "in modo d'un canzone populare." An onstage jazz band also makes an appearance in the nightclub scene of Act 2, while the opera's opening concerns that most contemporary of activities, a trip to the cinema. In addition, *Die Kathrin* makes prominent use of martial rhythms and fanfares, appropriate to the military setting of Act 1. As discussed in chapter 4, there are some striking resemblances between this martial musical language of *Die Kathrin* and *The Adventures of Robin Hood*.

The most arresting feature of Korngold's musical language is, as many have recognized, his command of melody, and this remains constant throughout his output. A typical Korngold melody is often characterized by intervals of the fourth, fifth, and seventh, as the love theme from *Another Dawn*, the accordion song from *The Sea Wolf*, Benjamin's theme from *Between Two Worlds*, and the "Jollity" theme from *The Adventures of Robin Hood* demonstrate (see example 2.3). The rising fourths are, as mentioned in chapter 1, part of Korngold's signature motif, the "motif of the cheerful heart," a melodic device that might have originated with Korngold's teacher Zemlinsky and his opera *Kleider machen Leute*.[27] *Die Kathrin*'s musical language, for example, is ultimately dominated by its use; its interlocking rising fourths are much in evidence at figure 34 in Act 1, for instance. The other motif that seems to occur regularly throughout the film scores is the death motif from *Die tote Stadt*.[28] First heard at the end of Act 1 when Paul's dead wife Marie appears to him, this descending chromatic recurs in *The Sea Hawk* as Thorpe and his men struggle through the Panama jungle, in *The Prince and the Pauper* when the young king is going to be murdered, in *The Sea Wolf* when Von Weyden has been shot, and, slightly altered, in *Between Two Worlds* as Anne and Henry begin to realize that they are, in fact, dead.

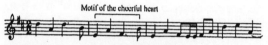

Example 2.3. Jollity Theme Melody

Korngold's approach to rhythm and meter was characterized by Friedhofer as a "sort of written-out rubato. It all sounded very free and relaxed, but it was all metronomically on the paper that way."[29] The scores are thus full of changes of time signature, a feature also common to the operas. At the beginning of Act 2, scene iii, in *Das Wunder der Heliane*, for example, or after figure 164 in "Ich ging zu ihm" from the same opera, the meter changes virtually every bar. In *The Adventures of Robin Hood*, a similar flexibility in the metrical structure is in evidence (see example 2.4).

Example 2.4. Flexible Meter in Cue 6A of *The Adventures of Robin Hood*

Korngold's approach to phraseology also seems to remain consistent across the genres, and he often chooses to extend phrases by an

extra beat, necessitating the changes in time signature seen in the operas and film scores. The *Vorspiel* to Act 2 of *Heliane*, for example,
extends cut time bars to 3/2 in order to lengthen the phrase in the same
manner employed in the tournament scene in *Robin Hood*. These exten-
sions allow Korngold to adjust music to fit the picture, but can be considered an intrinsic part of his style such that in the Symphony in F-
Sharp, entire parts of phrases can be optionally deleted without threatening the musical logic (see the Scherzo, two bars before 45 where six
and a half bars are marked "Vi=de").

Thematicism

Korngold's commitment to thematic structures in his scores is perhaps
his most obvious stylistic trait. While I would hesitate to apply the term
leitmotivic to the film scores, with its operatic and specifically
Wagnerian narrative associations, the musical structures of Korngold's
film scores are dominated by a number of recurring themes. This approach can be traced to Korngold's operatic output, beginning with
Violanta.

Utilizing a strong thematic design that could be termed leitmotivic,
each of the major characters in *Violanta* has their own theme:
Violanta's is first heard in the prelude—which also introduces Alfonso's melodious theme and anticipates the climactic scene of the opera—and she also has a separate leitmotiv to characterize her hatred of
Alfonso (much in the same way that the queen in *The Private Lives of
Elizabeth and Essex* has a distinct theme for her suffering); Violanta's
husband, Simone, has a martial theme that is noticeably separated from
the musical language of the two lovers, though where Violanta vows to
call him to murder Alfonso, she does so singing his music ("Dicht Aug
in Aug werd ich"). Like the transformations that occur in the film
scores, though, these themes can be subjected to changes to reflect the
drama: when Simone narrates the tale of Violanta's sister, Nerina, to
Giovanni Bracca, for example, the orchestra plays a darkened minor-
inflected version of Alfonso's music to indicate his complicity. Indeed,
only fragments of this theme are heard in his absence: when Violanta,
awaiting Alfonso, is asked by Barbara if she hears the sound of a boat,
Violanta, trembling, replies "Nein, nein. Ich hör nichts" (No, no. I hear
nothing), yet we hear a fragment from the beginning of Alfonso's
theme in the cor anglais. Even when Alfonso is on stage, we hear only
parts of his theme ("Sterben wollt ich oft"); not until Alfonso's out-

pouring of emotion before Violanta ("Doch was ich tat und wie ich immer fehlte") do we hear it complete, as in the prelude.

Das Wunder der Heliane could be said to epitomize the composer's dramatic abilities: its thematic and tonal structure certainly warrants the label 'leitmotivic,' and its rhythmic construction betrays the same complexities of rubato that would feature in his film scores. The Act 2 *Vorspiel*, with its repeated rising sequences, strident dissonances, swells, and syncopations could easily have been reused in one of the seascape scenes of *Captain Blood* or *The Sea Hawk*. Indeed, the Ruler, whose music this *Vorspiel* features, is such a deliciously evil character that Korngold's characterization of him seems, in the light of his later output, pure Hollywood. *Heliane* also features one of Korngold's most celebrated creations, the aria "Ich ging zu ihm." Heliane begins the aria by narrating the action of Act 1 in which she visits the stranger, condemned by her husband the Ruler to death because he has brought laughter to his realm. She falls in love with him and stands before him naked. Where she narrates "Er bat um meine Füße," for example, it parallels the Stranger's phrase "wie ewiges Licht rinnt über den Altar" from Act 1. The aria's move to F-sharp major—Korngold's favorite key and the tonal area symbolizing the power of love in opposition to the D minor of the Ruler—at the words "Doch schön war der Knabe" begins a chromatic melody that reveals itself at various points throughout the opera and dominates its musical structure.

Korngold was therefore completely at ease with complex thematic structures to support and enhance a narrative's dramatic construction. Unlike opera, though, where there may be large-scale musical processes at work independent of the libretto, the film score's structure is arguably far more dependent on the construction of the film itself. There is little evidence, for example, of any overarching tonal plan to the score of *The Adventures of Robin Hood*, nor any symbolism to the tonal areas used, as in *Heliane*. While Brendan Carroll has argued that *Captain Blood* stitched its individual cues into a symphonic whole that could almost be played without a break,[30] cues in *The Adventures of Robin Hood* frequently end and begin in remote keys that would prevent this kind of musical continuity. The structural continuity that is created in this, and other, film scores is therefore provided by the association of thematic material with characters, places, or concepts in the filmic narrative. This, to a degree, is dictated by the visual and aural structure of the edited film: the appearance or reference to these narrative elements triggers an associated musical sign in the underscore. A score like *Kings Row*, *Devotion*, or *The Sea Hawk* is full of identifiable

themes. Often they can be shortened to a 'head motif' that stands for
the whole theme: For instance, Drake's theme in *Kings Row*, like
Robin's theme in *The Adventures of Robin Hood* (see chapter 5) or
Thorpe's theme in *The Sea Hawk*, is often reduced to its first few notes.

As I have suggested, though I am wary of the term *leitmotiv*—
chiefly because, in contrast to Wagnerian opera, there are few moments
of overt narration in these films, nor do the themes develop in the same
way—I do not subscribe to the Eisler and Adorno viewpoint that regards the idea of leitmotiv in film scores as functioning merely on the
level of a redundant signpost, pointing out musically what is obvious
visually.[31] In the case of many of Korngold's scores, a subtle use of
thematicism is frequently operating at a level that transcends other visual or aural information.

In *Devotion* (produced in 1943 but not released until 1946), the
story of the Brontë sisters and a love triangle involving Charlotte
(Olivia de Havilland), Emily (Ida Lupino), and the local curate, Arthur
Nicholls (Paul Henreid), Emily's death scene provides an instance
where music seems to operate on a different narrative level. As Charlotte returns from London, where she has seen Nicholls and learned of
Emily's unrequited love for him, she tells Emily, on her deathbed, that
her own feelings for Nicholls have quite disappeared. While we might
suspect, along with Emily, that she lies to protect her dying sister's
feelings, the underscore exposes her white lie with an unambiguous
statement of the love theme. Similarly, Emily's dreams of an unidenti-
fied black rider on the moors are accompanied in the underscore by her
own theme in a strident minor-mode version: it is the figure of death
she seems to see, and the music associates it with her. Only when she
sees the rider's face does she realize what the music has already suggested to the audience, that she has "so little time" to finish her novel.
Music in these instances, it seems, is allied with an omniscient narrating voice; indeed the assumption that music always tells the truth is
something that Hollywood can play with as much as Wagnerian music-
drama.[32]

Thematicism thus not only provides the structure of Korngold's
scores but can also add extra levels of narrative complexity. In *The Sea
Hawk*, for example, the escape scene from the Spanish galleon is completely devoid of thematic references as Thorpe and his men work together to free themselves. Once their chains are removed, however, the
classless 'freedom' that the men enjoyed alongside Thorpe is replaced
by a reestablishment of the group's social hierarchy, and therefore by
the return of Thorpe's thematic material in the underscore. Nor do

themes remain the same; they are frequently altered, even developed, as part of the narrative's unfolding: In *The Adventures of Robin Hood*, for instance, the love theme and the theme for Richard and England are developed in a similar manner so that they become almost indistinguishable, while Robin's theme changes intervalically to resemble Richard's own theme (see chapter 5).

Use of Diegetic Music

As discussed later in chapters 4 and 5, *The Adventures of Robin Hood* makes little use of diegetic music, or at least seems to blur the distinction between the diegetic and nondiegetic, partly due to the restrictions placed on its musical content by MGM. In this regard it is relatively unusual within the context of Korngold's film score output. Many of Korngold's scores make prominent use of diegetic music, both newly composed material and preexisting classics. Like many aspects of Korngold's technique, this has its origins in the operas, several of which make use of the operatic equivalent of diegetic music, phenomenal song.

One of *Violanta*'s most important recurring musical ideas, for example, is the *totentanzlied* (literally "death dance song") or Carnival song, "Aus den Gräbern selbst die Toten," first sung by offstage voices at the beginning of the opera. This is an example of phenomenal song, as Carolyn Abbate would call it—singing that is heard *as singing* by the characters.[33] The song plays a crucial role in the drama that follows: Violanta asks Simone to kill Alfonso, but wants a moment alone with him first; the song signals the moment at which Simone is to rush in and commit the murder. "Glück, das mir verblieb" in *Die tote Stadt* is also phenomenal song that has an important dramatic function, though in character it is perhaps closer to the glorious diatonic B-major love duet from *Violanta* ("Reine Lieb, die ich suchte/Heisse Lust, der ich fluchte") than the Carnival song. Similarly, the presence of a musician as one of the main characters in *Die Kathrin* prompted Korngold to use more phenomenal song: the singing of François's little melody "Wenn Herz dem Herzen Treue hält"—'composed' on first sighting Kathrin, and 'sung' to her in Act 1—is the method by which Kathrin recognizes him in Act 2.

This interest of Korngold in the dramatic potential of phenomenal song can also be traced in the film scores' use of diegetic music, music that seems audible to the characters. In fact, three of the Korngold-scored films are directly concerned with fictional composers and thus dramatically feature the musical creations of their characters: *The Constant Nymph* (1943), about composer Lewis Dodd, traces the composition of a tone poem, *Tomorrow*; in *Escape Me Never* (released in 1947), it is composer Sebastien Dubrok's composition *Primavera* that illustrates the trials and tribulations of the artist; while in *Deception* (1946), the composer Hollenius and his Cello Concerto, to be performed by Paul Henreid's character, prove central to the plot. Indeed such is their importance that Robbert van der Lek regards the vocal compositions in *The Constant Nymph* and *Escape Me Never*, along with "La Paloma" in *Juarez*, as 'leitmelodies' that bear direct comparison with the dramatic function of the Carnival song in *Violanta*.[34]

Deception also features classical extracts performed diegetically, including the Haydn D-major Cello Concerto and Beethoven's Seventh Symphony. Indeed, one of the most effective pieces of underscoring in the film uses the opening of Schubert's Eighth Symphony, supposedly being played by the orchestra off-camera, as Christine and Karel are reunited. The eventual tragic outcome set in motion by this meeting is perfectly suggested by the nervous, menacing character of the Schubert, despite the joy of the characters at finding each other again; even the second subject of the first movement seems perfectly synchronized with the tender words exchanged. Similarly, *Devotion* includes Johann Strauss II and Haydn in its ball scene, piano pieces by Schubert and Chopin, and a ballet by Pugni, while *Anthony Adverse* features an extract from Monteverdi's *Orfeo*. *Kings Row*'s principal character, Parris, is an accomplished pianist, thus providing an opportunity for him to play the Beethoven "Pathétique" sonata. As with *Deception* where Christine performs the "Appassionata" sonata diegetically, Korngold incorporates Beethoven's thematic material into the underscore, thus integrating diegetic and nondiegetic music and adding yet another musical voice to the Korngold persona. In *Between Two Worlds*, it is Henry's music, previously heard on the gramophone as he commits suicide, and performed by him on the piano, that continues in the underscore. In this instance, the blurring of diegetic and nondiegetic music is particularly apt, since the characters are traveling "between two worlds." Henry can claim that this is "a world in which there is room for music" to the extent that the sound of breaking glass in the mortal life leaks into his world as musical chords.

Demarcation of Narrative Space

Korngold was particularly adept at providing a sense of narrative space in his music, supplying not only information of geographical or temporal relevance but also outlining spatial relationship between characters and locations.

The leakage of narrative space signified by the glass-breaking chords of *Between Two Worlds*, for instance, is effective precisely because boundaries have been clearly created. The calm interior of Henry's apartment as he prepares to commit suicide is thus musically contrasted with Anne's frantic dash through the streets as she rushes to prevent him. Such cross-cutting between scenes of calm and activity is much in evidence in the attack on the treasure caravan sequence in *The Adventures of Robin Hood* (see chapter 5). Similarly, the escape scene from *The Sea Hawk* contrasts the calm routine world of the guards on deck with the intense activity of the escapees struggling below. The battle scene earlier in the same film also makes particular use of musical devices to demarcate the spatial location of the two ships. The *Albatross*'s hail to the Spanish ship, for example, is accompanied by a trumpet fanfare that is 'answered' by a musical echo, while the *Albatross*'s theme defines the space of the ship, so that when the camera shot changes to a different location on board, the theme modulates in tonality. While Korngold may not synchronize his music as closely with the visuals as Max Steiner did, there are still numerous instances where Korngold's scores engage in so-called Mickey Mousing. Parris throwing a stone into the pond in *Kings Row* is accompanied by a harp glissando, while in *The Sea Wolf*, for instance, Dr. Prescott's fall from the mast is mimicked in the score's falling scales; *The Adventures of Robin Hood* is no exception in this regard, as chapter 5 reveals.

Korngold's scores also provide geographical information, despite the widely held view that he composed in an 'international' style that avoided any overt ethnic stereotypes. Kevin Donnelly has recently written:

> One of the striking aspects of this outstanding series of musical scores [*Captain Blood, The Adventures of Robin Hood, The Private Lives of Elizabeth and Essex*, and *The Sea Hawk*] is that they eschew any attempt to evoke the English (and colonial) settings or concerns through music, and deal in an 'international' musical style.[35]

This seems a difficult statement to support. *The Sea Hawk* perfectly evokes a colonial sense of 'Otherness' in its percussion-dominated

Panama sequence, and its sinuous Spanish theme with Habanera rhythms and ornamentation is clearly opposed to the normative 'English' world of regal fanfares. Similarly, *Captain Blood*'s sense of colonial Otherness is aided by the exotically colored theme for Port Royal, which is contrasted with the rather stately and conventionally orchestrated theme associated with the Englishman, Willoughby. While these films' evocation of England may not make use of Vaughan Williams-style folk arrangement or modal harmonies, Marian's theme in *The Adventures of Robin Hood* is, as revealed in chapter 4, based on an old ballad tune, and as argued in chapter 3, Hollywood's evocation of 'old England' can often be regarded as allegorical.

In terms of aiding the temporal location of the narrative, Korngold famously argued against the adaptation of his musical style, remarking that the "characters [in *Elizabeth and Essex*] speak the English spoken today. Why then should the composer use 'thou' and 'thee' and 'thine' if the dialogue does not?"[36] Yet a large number of the films that Korngold scored deal with historical subjects, albeit a highly mythologized form of history. As Caryl Flinn has argued, Korngold's scores play a large role in creating this nostalgic mythologized atmosphere, offering us an "assuring regalness and stability."[37] There are, however, instances of diegetic music, particularly in the coronation scene of *The Prince and the Pauper* or the Elizabethan songs of *The Sea Hawk* and *The Private Lives of Elizabeth and Essex*, where Korngold approaches a pseudo-archaic style. Angela's song in *Anthony Adverse* is similarly stylistically appropriate to its cultural and historical milieu, especially when played by the local town band.[38] In that sense, it bears certain resemblance to the stylistically apposite instances of phenomenal song heard in the operas, with Marietta's lute song in particular standing out as phenomenal precisely because of its stylistic incongruity with much of the rest of *Die tote Stadt*'s musical language.

Korngold's Self-Borrowings and the Idea of 'Intertextuality'

Deception is a particularly interesting film in that the character of Hollenius, in some musical sense at least, stands as the on-screen representative of Korngold, as the composer "who combines the melody of yesterday with the rhythm of today." Peter Franklin has examined the film, placing it within the larger dialectic of modernism and mass culture, in which the 'authentic classical' music of Hollenius and the diegetic classical extracts are placed in opposition to the deceptive, sentimental 'woman's' music of the underscore.[39] Christine's murder of Hollenius can thus be seen in terms of a feminized mass culture dispatching patriarchal European high-art culture. It would be too simplistic to claim that, despite Korngold's input into the script, Hollenius is merely a ventriloquist's dummy through which the real composer speaks—with all his apparent anxieties about his status as a high-art composer engaged in popular music[40]—yet a throwaway comment by Hollenius perhaps reveals much about Korngold's attitude to creativity. Shortly before he is murdered by Christine, Hollenius appears in the depths of despair, remarking that Christine should try composing a piece herself and see how it sounds after listening to Beethoven. Could such a comment be traced to Korngold's input on the script? Does it reveal a Bloomian anxiety of influence?

Certainly, Korngold's ready wit was frequently applied to issues of creative originality. Bronislaw Kaper's story about Korngold's humorous put-down of Sigmund Romberg, a film composer renowned for his borrowings from other composers, perhaps attests to a certain sensitivity. Kaper, Korngold, and a young inexperienced composer are shown Romberg's extensive library of musical scores. "My god," says the young man, "is all this music his?" "Not *yet*," quips Korngold in return.[41] Similarly, the oft-quoted exchange between Korngold and Steiner when they passed each other around the time of *Of Human Bondage* bears repeating:

> "Erich, we've both been working at Warners for ten years now" (Korngold nodded and winced) "and during that time, it seems to me, your music has gotten worse and worse whereas mine has gotten better and better—now why do you suppose that is?"
>
> Without pausing for breath, Korngold replied, "That's easy Steiner; it's because you have been stealing from me and I have been stealing from you!"[42]

While I do not wish to suggest that Korngold meant the remark seriously, it perhaps reveals a certain preoccupation with issues of musical borrowing that deserves attention.

Film composers are perhaps understandably more aware of charges of 'plagiarism' or threats to a romantic aesthetic of originality than other composers working in the concert hall, since they are forced to justify their artistic status in the face of attacks by cultural critics like Adorno. Bernard Herrmann's vitriolic and, it seems, inaccurate denial of his own self-borrowings are particularly revealing in this regard.[43]

Korngold, too, was by all accounts acutely aware of these issues and took pains to have his title card on *Captain Blood* changed to "musical arrangements by" in case it was thought he was taking credit for the Liszt extracts he used (see below). He was also sensitive about the accidental allusion made to Sibelius's *Finlandia* in Randy's theme from *Kings Row*, a similarity pointed out by Hugo Friedhofer.[44] Korngold immediately wanted to change it, but the postproduction process was too far along to allow such a large change to the thematic structure. Korngold also seemed to be wary of 'competing' with other composers: he refused to work on a 1926 production of Schiller's *Turandot* with Max Reinhardt for the Salzburg Festival when he learned that Puccini's opera was to première that year.[45]

Alongside this distancing of himself from musical borrowings or allusions, Korngold also apparently made a startling confession to Friedhofer about Dukas's *Ariane et Barbe-Bleu*:

> I remember once [Korngold] spoke of Dukas's unjustly neglected opera *Ariane et Barbe-Bleu* in glowing terms, and saying, at the conclusion of an hour-long eulogy, peppered with excerpts from the score (which he played on the piano from memory) that he "had been living off Ariane for many years." Be that as it may, the fact remains that whatever he borrowed became transmuted in the crucible of his enormous individuality, and the end product was always pure Korngold...tune detecting is, after all, a childish game played by young music students, unimaginative critics, and the second violinist on the next-to-last desk in any orchestra.[46]

Certainly Korngold's love of augmented triads could be potentially traced to the whole-tone language of *Ariane*.

Whether or not Korngold was always entirely serious in his comments concerning musical creativity, it is clear his musical output can be investigated within the context of theories of intertextuality—theories that state that "all Texts speak of other Texts," and thus that "all music speaks of other music." In other words, the meanings we read in any Text are dependent on the existence of other Texts. Fixed boundaries between discrete identifiable Texts thus disappear, and the concept of the intertext arises; meaning is mediated through the interplay of signs achieved in the intertextual space. All music forms part of an intertext by dint of common harmonic and rhythmic languages, and the term could therefore cover a multitude of relationships, a network of meanings accrued over a lifetime of musical interactions. While the theoretical implications of intertextuality in the search for meaning are perhaps most relevant to the reading of a film score, as offered in chapter 5, I raise the issue now because there are numerous instances where common material can be found in both Korngold's film scores and his operas and concert works that extend much further than the constant use of the motif of the cheerful heart or the death motif from *Die tote Stadt*.[47] This 'musical borrowing' must therefore be considered a major facet of his compositional style. Similarly, the stylistic resemblances between certain John Williams scores of the 1970s and Korngold's music could be discussed within the scope of this concept. The heroic title theme of *Superman* (1978), for example, bears a striking resemblance to the rising fifth and neighboring notes of Emily's theme from *Devotion*, and the leaping seventh of *Kings Row*'s main title.

The notion of 'intertextuality' was first conceptualized by cultural critics such as Julia Kristeva and Roland Barthes in the 1960s and 1970s and has long been applied to literary theory. Harold Bloom's theory of the anxiety of influence in poetry, developed to explain how 'strong' authors grapple with and defeat their predecessors, is thus, to some degree, a theory of intertextuality.[48] In more recent years, such ideas have also been applied in musicology, with Kevin Korsyn's work on the anxiety of influence in Chopin and Brahms causing a flurry of interest in the musicological community, especially in light of its apparent reinscription of Bloomian patriarchal values.[49] Korsyn's work, in casting Brahms as a composer who wrestles successfully with the strong precursor of Chopin, relegates Reger to the status of a 'secondary man':

> A certain lack of resistance vitiates Reger's arabesques; compared to Chopin's, Reger's figurations seem flaccid, meandering, directionless. Consequently, although not without charm, it is weak....
> Reger's piece [*Träume am Kamin*, op. 43] fails on its own terms; he wrestles unsuccessfully with the Berceuse, and weakly misreads and reduces Chopin.[50]

This notion of influence as a potential threat to artistic achievement is perhaps reflected in Friedhofer's comments on childish "tune detecting." Less value-laden approaches to ideas of intertextuality, though, can be seen in Christopher Reynolds's recent study of allusive practices in nineteenth-century composers, such as Mendelssohn and Schumann, though he stresses intentionality as an important element in his definition of allusion.[51] The concept has also received particular attention in Michael L. Klein's 2005 book, *Intertextuality in Western Art Music*,[52] though Klein is keen to distinguish concepts of influence, which requires intent or a historical placement of works, from intertextuality, which allows for unconscious allusions and the historical reversal of texts, such that Bach can allude to Chopin:

> Through the intertext with Chopin's C-minor etude, I assert outrageously that these repetitions [in the C-major prelude from Bach's *Well-Tempered Clavier*] exist to make clear just that connection between the two texts [that the prelude tropes the C-minor etude by shattering the registral arches played by both hands]. Thus Chopin is the precursor to Bach because he asks us to hear the earlier composer's prelude in a new way. The prelude as newly-heard has no existence prior to Chopin's etude.[53]

While the self-borrowings evident in the Korngold text tend to work to a chronological pattern, with material used in earlier film scores turning up in the post-1946 concert works, this is not always the case. Yet, as Klein argues, once we engage with the concept of intertextuality in our search for musical meaning, the notion of chronology becomes irrelevant; the Korngoldian Text thus transcends any mere chronological concerns. Nor need this discussion be confined to deliberate borrowings or quotation: the allusion to George M. Cohan's World War II patriotic song "Over There" in Korngold's Symphony in F-Sharp is not generally acknowledged to be intentional,[54] though as the symphony is dedicated to Franklin D. Roosevelt, it seems entirely apposite.[55]

The following discussion will therefore embrace both the thematic ideas that originated in the film scores and material that was first heard in the concert hall as constituting part of the Korngoldian Text. Followed to its logical conclusion, this illustrates the potential for rich discussions of the concert works based upon the meanings brought in via the musical borrowings from film scores.

Preexisting Material Used in Film Scores

Of particular relevance to *Robin Hood* were Korngold's experiences with *Captain Blood*. Faced with a tight deadline, he resorted to using extracts from Liszt's symphonic poem *Prometheus*, a decision that resulted in his credit reading "musical arrangements by," at his own request. The orchestrator Hugo Friedhofer refers to this incident in his oral history:

I don't know whether Korngold was tired, or what, but anyway, he decided that except for an introduction to [the duel sequence], a play into the actual duel, and a play-off at the end, we adapted something from a symphonic poem of Franz Liszt called "Prometheus." It had a fugue. And fugues make an excellent background for duels, because that's the conflict—one voice against the other. I think I still have a miniature score of the Liszt piece, with the markings in it that we discussed the night I went over to his house, at about eight o'clock in the evening, and left around midnight and went home and orchestrated. The copyist picked it up in the morning, and that afternoon it was recorded.[56]

© 1974 American Film Institute

Yet Friedhofer fails to mention that it wasn't just this one passage that made use of the Liszt, and his word has generally been accepted without any further investigation by commentators.[57] In fact, another sequence in the score extracts a sizable portion from *Prometheus*: when the town of Port Royal is attacked by pirates, the score consists entirely of extracts from the Liszt. In addition, as Kathryn Kalinak points out, the score also makes use of another Liszt symphonic poem, *Mazeppa*.[58] Though at times it can be difficult to hear the score under the diegetic noise of battle, the source of the music in these sequences is summarized in table 2.1.

Table 2.1. Liszt's *Prometheus* and *Mazeppa* in *Captain Blood*

Approx. timing (Region 1 DVD)	Visual action	Source
0:47:11	Bishop strikes Blood.	*Prometheus* bs. 1–6.
0:47:16	Watch tower calls "Pirates. Spanish Pirates!"	*Prometheus* bs. 5–6.
0:47:31	Bishop joins sentry at the tower; shot of the town and narration card "The Timely Interruption..."; shot of Spanish ship.	*Prometheus* bs. 241–249, 283–291.
0:47:50	Battery of Port Royal and Spanish ship exchange fire.	*Prometheus* bs. 292–298.
0:47:57–0:48:26	Wide shot of Port Royal and Spanish ships; shot of townsfolk running; scenes of battle.	*Prometheus* bs. 78–101.

Table 2.1. Liszt's *Prometheus* and *Mazeppa* in *Captain Blood* (continued)

Approx. timing (Region 1 DVD)	Visual action	Source
0:49:12–0:49:34	Spanish ship firing; soldiers disembarking and looting.	*Mazeppa* 11 after O to 4 before Q (cutting 7–10 before Q).
0:56:00–0:56:30	Cheering and more firing of Blood's canons at Spaniards.	*Prometheus* bs. 62–67, 78–96.
1:24:39	Blood draws his sword; Levasseur does likewise while one of his men tries to restrain him; he replies "C'est mon affair."	*Prometheus.* Score based on fugue subject (bs. 161–164).
1:24:53	Duel.	*Prometheus* bs. 161–238 extensively reorchestrated to be "gutsier."[59]
1:26:13	Levasseur falls; lull in the fighting.	
1:26:24	Duel resumes.	*Prometheus* bs. 239–240.
1:26:48	Duel resumes.	*Prometheus* bs. 243–244.
1:45:24	French ships seen through telescope; scenes of battle.	*Mazeppa* beginning to letter B.
1:46:20–1:46:30	"Stand by ready to fire"; scenes of battle.	*Mazeppa* letter C to 7 after C.
1:49:04	Blood orders the wreckage cleared; scenes of battle.	*Mazeppa* beginning to 8 after C.
1:50:33	Blood orders musketeers to the prow; scenes of battle.	*Mazeppa* letter B to 7 after C.
1:51:10–1:52:07	Blood gives order to prepare to swing across on ropes; grappling hooks are thrown across and ships pulled together.	*Mazeppa* bar before D to 29 after D; 30 before E to 19 before E (repeated).

This cut-and-stitch technique with existing pieces of concert music is something we usually associate more with the 'music factories' of Universal and the smaller studios, yet Korngold makes further use of this approach in *The Adventures of Robin Hood*. Perhaps concerned about the difficulty of scoring what he regarded as a "ninety percent action picture," Korngold decided to use portions of his own 1919 concert overture *Sursum Corda* and a cue from his arrangement of Leo

Fall's operetta *Rosen aus Florida* entitled "Miß Austria" to help (see chapter 4 for a full discussion of how these pieces were adapted).

Less obvious musical self-borrowings from earlier concert works and operas also occurred in a number of other film scores. A phrase from *Sursum Corda* appears to turn up, slightly altered, at the end of the titles sequence for *Another Dawn*,[60] while the scene at the Belgian school in *Devotion*, for example, appears to reference the opening of *Die Kathrin*. Another operatic reference is found in *Between Two Worlds*'s love music, which has strong links with "Ich ging zu ihm" from Act 2 of *Das Wunder der Heliane*.[61] Benjamin's theme from the same film, on the other hand, seems to have originated rather appropriately from "Sterbelied" (a song of death) in the *Vier Lieder des Abschieds* of 1920–1921. Indeed "Gefasster Abschied" from the same set has certain melodic features in common with the title music from *Between Two Worlds*. Given the film's subject matter, the transition between death and the afterlife, the appropriateness of referencing a set of songs concerned with farewells and an opera about resurrection is striking.

In *The Private Lives of Elizabeth and Essex* (1939), eight bars of the overture were taken—appropriately enough given the subject matter—from a piece written in 1916 for the Austrian empress called *Kaiserin Zita-Hymne*.[62] Similarly, the satirical song sung by Olivia de Havilland's character to the queen, Brendan Carroll argues, was composed for a Max Reinhardt Workshop in 1937; it was later published with its original Shakespearean text, "O Mistress Mine" from *Twelfth Night*, as part of the Op. 29 *Narrenlieder* (Songs of a Clown).[63]

Anthony Adverse (1936), *The Prince and the Pauper* (1937), and *Juarez* (1939) all feature material that was published as part of the Violin Concerto Op. 35 in 1945, yet Korngold began working on this concerto in 1937, before *Juarez* was scored. It is therefore conceivable that what became the love theme of Maximillian and Carlota in *Juarez* was originally intended as the concerto first movement's second subject; it certainly features prominently in the 1945 revised version of the concerto. *The Sea Hawk* (1940), like *Elizabeth and Essex*, features a preexisting song that is sung diegetically. As Brendan Carroll has revealed, this song—which Korngold later published as "Alt Spanisch" in the *Fünf Lieder* Op. 38—was composed for the Op. 9 *Sechs Einfache Lieder* under the title "Das Mädchen."[64] The song is sung in the film by Dona Maria (played by Brenda Marshall) and its opening bars also double as her theme in the underscore; "Das Mädchen/Alt Spanisch" thus pervades much of the score.

Allusions to (future) film scores can also be found in Korngold's
Piano Concerto for the Left Hand (1923), the first such concerto com-
missioned by Paul Wittgenstein, before those by Ravel (1929–1930)
and Prokofiev (1931). The three bars before figure 2 seem to have some
affinity with the duel from *The Sea Hawk*, while the flute/piccolo melody at figure 6 has much in common with the main melody of *Escape
Me Never*. Even the opening of the concerto shares its rhythm and melodic shape with both the opening of King Richard's theme and the
love theme from *The Adventures of Robin Hood* (see chapter 5).

Aside from the Beethoven references found in *Kings Row* and *Deception* (following the diegetic performances of his piano sonatas), and
the unintentional Sibelius allusion in *Kings Row* mentioned above, musical material 'by other composers' can be found referenced in many of
Korngold's scores. *Juarez*, for instance, makes use of the preexisting
song "La Paloma," said to be a favorite of Empress Carlota, though in
this case the 'borrowing' is openly acknowledged.[65] *Another Dawn*
appears to allude to the Gershwin song "The Man I Love" at certain
points, most notably when Denny and Julia say goodnight after their
first significant conversation,[66] and *The Prince and the Pauper* seems
to allude to Johann Strauss II's *Kaiser-Walzer* when Tom Canty is talk-
ing to Father Andrew.[67] In addition, Kathryn Kalinak has also suggested that the fanfares heard in *Captain Blood*, when Blood raises the
French flag to fool his enemies, are a variation on the bugle call from
Bizet's *Carmen*.[68] There is also the suggestion of an allusion to the
"Tanzlied" from Richard Strauss's *Also Sprach Zarathustra* at the end
of *Between Two Worlds*; as this score also alludes to Korngold's own
Abschiedslieder—one of which ("Mond, so gehst du wieder auf") also
seems to share a similar opening with "September" from Strauss's later
Vier Letzte Lieder (1948)—this web of allusion, intentional or acciden-
tal, seems entirely appropriate.

Intertextuality between Film Scores

In addition to referencing existing concert works or operas, many of
Korngold's scores also reference his earlier film scores. *The Sea Hawk*,
for example, makes use of material sketched for the abandoned Max
Reinhardt film *Danton* in 1936[69] and an orchestral sequence called
"The Flood" that Korngold provided, without screen credit, for *The
Green Pastures* (1936).[70] *The Sea Hawk*'s distinctive B-flat-major E-
major chord sequence, repeated an octave lower and heard during
Thorpe's escape scene, originates in the score for *A Midsummer Night's*

Dream when Bottom discovers his ass's head, while the Panama sequence seems to reuse material written for the Irish sequence in *The Private Lives of Elizabeth and Essex*: foreign 'Otherness' can be Irish or Central American, it seems. Moreover, the Spanish ambush of Thorpe's men in Panama uses material from battle scenes in *Juarez*, while much of the dominant preparation before "Strike for the Shores of Dover" is taken directly from the same film, as Juarez's men decide to attack the French.

The opening of the main theme from *Elizabeth and Essex*, with its rising fourth and fifth followed by a descent, shares much in common with the main theme from *Kings Row*. More overtly perhaps, Thackeray's theme in *Devotion* is, in fact, the theme heard in *Captain Blood* as Willoughby and Arabella Bishop stroll the decks of a ship returning from England; it will eventually be heard triumphantly as the Union Jack is raised aboard Blood's ship. The term "intertextual graft" is used in Peter Brunette and David Willis's 1989 book, *Screen/Play: Derrida and Film Theory* in connection with the appearance of the same actor in different films, and its resulting effect on meaning.[71] To hear Thackeray/Willoughby's theme in *Devotion* in scenes featuring Olivia de Havilland (who also played Arabella in *Captain Blood*) thus helps reinforce the intertextual graft created by de Havilland's presence in both films.

Perhaps the most interesting case of this phenomenon occurs in *Deception* as part of the Hollenius Cello Concerto. As the concerto is being rehearsed, we hear part of the work that quotes from *The Private Lives of Elizabeth and Essex*,[72] namely, the theme for the queen's sorrow heard as she laments the fact that a monarch is not allowed to love. The camera in *Deception* shows us Christine (Bette Davis) looking pensive, worried about how the rehearsal involving her husband and ex-lover is progressing. The presence of this theme in the music, however, provides another explanation: Bette Davis played the queen in *Elizabeth and Essex*, and her pensiveness seems to cross the boundaries between Texts, as if the music reminds her of her unhappiness in the earlier film and her inability to love freely.[73] A fragment of Essex's march from the opening scene of *Elizabeth and Essex* can also be heard in *Kings Row* as Parris rushes to Drake's house after his romantic liaison with Cassie; no doubt there are many more of these self-borrowings or self-allusions littered throughout the scores, a comprehensive investigation of which is beyond the scope of this study.

Film Scores in Later Concert Works

The Korngold Text extends far beyond the use of earlier concert
works/operas in the film scores, though, or the use of common musical
material in different films. When Korngold returned to composing for
the concert hall after the end of the war, his works made numerous references to the film scores. Mention has already been made of the songs
from *The Private Lives of Elizabeth and Essex* and *The Sea Hawk* that
were later extracted and published; similarly, other pieces of diegetic
music were later published, though with revisions. Thus the tone poem
Tomorrow for mezzo-soprano, women's chorus, and orchestra from
The Constant Nymph became Op. 33, and the Cello Concerto composed
for *Deception* was published as Korngold's Op. 37. Other concert
works, though, conceived entirely as such, feature thematic material
that can be traced to the film scores. In fact, virtually every one of his
post-Hollywood concert works makes some reference to film music
material, providing rich opportunity for fascinating hermeneutic discussion of musical meanings in these so-called autonomous forms.

The Violin Concerto—composed between 1937 and 1939, and
substantially revised in 1945—uses, in addition to the love music from
Juarez, the love theme from *Another Dawn* (1937). This became the
opening movement's principal subject, though again it may have been
sketched for the violin concerto first and then reused for the film score.
The second movement ("Romance") adapts love music from *Anthony
Adverse* (1936), and the finale takes much of its material from *The
Prince and the Pauper* (1937). The question of whether the film scores
or sketches for the concerto came first is, as has been intimated above,
somewhat irrelevant if we embrace the notion of intertextuality; it is
enough to recognize that the concerto shares material with some of the
film scores and is thus part of the same 'Text.'

Works that definitely postdate the scores from which some of their
material is taken include: the Third String Quartet, Op. 34; *Fünf Lieder*,
Op. 38; the *Symphonic Serenade*, Op. 39; the Symphony in F-Sharp,
Op. 40; and *Sonett für Wien*, Op. 41. The Third String Quartet's slow
movement "*Sostenuto*—like a folk tune" is based on music from *The
Sea Wolf* (including the accordion 'song' and Ruth's theme),[74] while
the trio of the Scherzo uses Bunny the vicar's theme from *Between Two
Worlds*,[75] and the finale borrows Miss Branwell's theme from *Devotion*.[76] The sisters' theme from *Devotion* (first heard in the title music)
also provided the material for "Glückwunsch," the first of *Fünf Lieder*.
This set of songs has numerous overlaps with the film scores: "Der

Kranke" uses a motif from *Juarez*; "Alt Englisch" was a song written for, but never used in, *The Private Lives of Elizabeth and Essex*;[77] and "Alt Spanisch" is, of course, Maria's song from *The Sea Hawk*. The two major orchestral works also abound with film score references. The Mahlerian *Lento religioso* of the *Symphonic Serenade* for strings, composed in 1947–1948, quotes Brother Francois's mournful chorale theme from *Anthony Adverse*,[78] while the second theme of the Finale is taken from the first love scene between Blood and Arabella in *Captain Blood*. Similarly, Korngold's magnificent Symphony in F-Sharp takes as its slow movement's principal idea Essex's theme from *Elizabeth and Essex*, while at figure 84 the love theme from *Captain Blood* is heard. At figure 86 a section is taken from the African-set part of *Anthony Adverse* when Anthony goes looking for Brother Francois,[79] and the Symphony's finale uses the Grandmother's theme from *Kings Row* (at figures 116–118 and 141–143). Finally, the piano part of *Sonett für Wien* is based on the main theme from *Escape Me Never*.[80]

   The Adventures of Robin Hood is no exception in this regard. Material from the score makes a disguised, yet immediately recognizable, appearance in Korngold's last published opus, the *Theme and Variations*, written in the summer of 1953 for school orchestra performance. The final variation at bar 187 is strongly reminiscent of cue 10E in the film (the coronation procession). This film score is therefore part of a Text that stretches from 1919, when *Sursum Corda* was written, to 1953 at the very least. As will be seen in chapter 4, Korngold's research into old Robin Hood ballads and use of "Summer Is Icumen In" arguably pushes this earlier date much further back.

3

THE HISTORICAL AND CRITICAL CONTEXT OF *ROBIN HOOD*

In the same way that a Korngold score can be understood as part of a series of musical Texts, *The Adventures of Robin Hood*, as a complete film, shares features in common with other film treatments and literary forms of the legend and derives meaning from its place in the swashbuckler genre. It also acquires significance from its position within a historical Text, namely, the political climate of 1937–1938. In addressing possible readings of the film, then, an appreciation of these various historical and critical contexts is required.

The Legend of Robin Hood

The origins of Robin Hood as a historical or purely literary figure have been endlessly debated by both historians and literary scholars. It is not my intention to provide an in-depth discussion of the issues here, but rather to address briefly some of the factors that impact the 1938 Warner Bros. treatment of the legend; readers interested in learning more might like to consult Stephen Knight's edited compendium *Robin Hood: An Anthology of Scholarship and Criticism*.[1]

While historical references to a Robin Hood character, or one similarly named, can be found as early as the thirteenth century, the first significant collection of Robin Hood tales, *The Gest of Robyn Hode*, was assembled in fifteenth century, probably after 1450. The *Gest* includes such familiar staples as the character of Little John (associated with Robin from very early on), the archery tournament, Robin's meeting with the king in Sherwood, and Sir Guy of Gisbourne. By the end of the fifteenth century, Robin also appears in dramatic and semi-dramatic guise in plays and May-games. While the character of Robin is, in the ballad tradition, a yeoman, two plays by Anthony Munday published at the turn of the seventeenth century turn him into Robert, Earl of Huntington.

Both Friar Tuck and Maid Marian are missing from the earliest tales. While Friar Tuck as a historical figure or alias for any disturber of the peace can be traced back to Henry V's reign in the form of the parson Robert Stafford, he is first associated with Robin's band of men about 1475. Marian, by contrast, is a purely literary figure and originates in a French pastoral play, *Robin et Marian* of about 1283 by Adam de la Halle; it is not until the May-games of around 1500, where she becomes the May Queen to Robin's King, that she is associated with Robin Hood. Her appearance in the plays of Munday a century later is as the character Matilda, thus identifying her with one of the semi-mythical Matildes persecuted by King John.

Further additions to the legend, notably Robin's status as protector of the poor, began to appear in the sixteenth and seventeenth centuries, and by the time Joseph Ritson's anthology of poems, songs, and ballads appeared in 1795, its introductory 'history' could codify Robin's chivalric character:

> [i]t is to be remembered...[that] he took away the goods of rich men only; never killing any person, unless he was attacked or resisted: that he would not suffer a woman to be maltreated; nor ever took anything from the poor, but charitably fed them with the wealth he drew from the abbots.[2]

Ritson further describes the character of Robin, or Robert Fitzooth, as a man of exemplary piety (in spite of his resistance to the clergy) who was "active, brave, prudent, patient; possessed of uncommon bodily strength and considerable military skill; just, generous, benevolent, faithful, and beloved or revered by his followers or adherents for his excellent and amiable qualities."[3]

Ritson's anthology prompted a wave of Romantic creativity; like the Elizabethan and Jacobean playwrights before them, the poets and novelists of the nineteenth century fundamentally altered the legend. Sir Walter Scott's novel *Ivanhoe* (1819), for example, introduces the idea of Saxon resistance to Norman oppression—a divide which the marriage of Ivanhoe and Rowena, attended by high-born Normans and Saxons alike, serves to mend, and a conflict which became a crucial part of the myth as it appeared on screen. Though the yeoman Robin

Hood—or Locksley as he's known for much of Scott's novel—is merely a supporting player in the drama, the character of the disinherited knight Wilfred of Ivanhoe is very much in the mold that Ritson established for Robin. Ivanhoe is romantically chivalrous and rushes to defend the honor of Rebecca the Jewess, accused of sorcery by the anti-Semitic Templars. In fact, the novel's complex engagement with the anti-Semitism prevalent in England at the time of its setting leads to an ambivalent conclusion whereby Rebecca and her father are forced to leave England: social harmony, it seems, comes at a price. *Ivanhoe* also introduces the iconic image of Robin splitting the arrow at an archery tournament, and—as with the early ballads—makes much of disguise as a narrative device: King Richard returns to England disguised as an errant knight; Ivanhoe first appears as a palmer, and later under the name El Desdichado; and Wamba, the jester, disguises himself as a friar to gain the freedom of his master. Perhaps most crucially for the 1938 Warner Bros. film, though, is the idea, outlined by Graham Tulloch, that Scott connected events in *Ivanhoe* with the turbulent events of the Peterloo massacre[4]—that writing about a mythic past was a way of commenting upon the present. As we shall discover, this idea has particular resonance for an interpretation of *The Adventures of Robin Hood*.

Also dating from the period of *Ivanhoe* was Thomas Love Peacock's novel *Maid Marian* (1822).[5] Ritson's history acknowledges that there is no mention of Marian in the early sources, yet he maintains her importance to the Elizabethan plays, and her newfound status is perhaps reflected in this short comic novel. Marian is the beautiful Matilda Fitzwater who, at the novel's outset, is about to be wed to the noble Robert of Fitz-Ooth, Earl of Locksley and Huntingdon, when Robert is declared an outlaw for hunting the king's deer by Sir Ralph Montfaucon. The plucky Matilda, who is handy with bow and arrow, joins Robert, or Robin Hood, in Sherwood and is rechristened Marian by Friar Tuck. The group establishes six principles of society—Legitimacy, Equity, Hospitality, Chivalry, Chastity, and Courtesy—and vows to restore the natural balance of power. Richard returns to England to pardon Robin and his men, and restore Robin to his earldom, while Prince John and Sir Ralph are defeated.

While Marian's role seemingly grew steadily, Howard Pyle's lavishly illustrated book for children, *The Merry Adventures of Robin Hood of Great Renown in Nottinghamshire* (1893),[6] barely mentions her. Yet, the other main set pieces of the legend, mostly derived from Ritson's anthology, are all present, namely: Robin's encounter with

Little John and their fight with staffs; Robin splitting an arrow to show his skill; a disguised Robin winning a golden arrow at an archery tournament; Robin's rescue of Will Stutely from the clutches of the Sheriff of Nottingham; Robin forcing the Curtal Friar of Fountain Abbey to carry him across the river on his back; the rich Bishop of Hereford forced to part with two-thirds of his treasure in return for a feast in Sherwood; Robin fighting and killing Sir Guy of Gisbourne, and disguising himself as Sir Guy in order to rescue Little John; and the return of King Richard disguised as a friar.

Robin Hood on Film

Given the popularity of the legend in literary genres, it is perhaps unsurprising that the twentieth century's newest art form should embrace the subject of Robin Hood. A number of silent films were produced in both Britain and America between 1908 and 1913, but it was the 1922 Douglas Fairbanks version that cemented the outlaw's place in cinematic history.

The most expensive film yet made, at over $1.5 million, *Robin Hood* was produced by Fairbanks's United Artists and mostly bankrolled by its larger-than-life producer and star. Fairbanks plays Robin as the noble Earl of Huntingdon, who departs for the Crusades with King Richard (Wallace Beery) while a scheming Prince John (Sam de Grasse), with the help of Sir Guy of Gisbourne (Paul Dickey) and the High Sheriff of Nottingham (William Lovery), initiates a reign of tyranny over England. Huntingdon returns when Marian (Enid Bennett), his betrothed, sends him word of Prince John's treachery. He transforms into Robin Hood, while his squire (Alan Hale) becomes Little John, to lead the outlaws of Sherwood Forest in revolt.

The film, at nearly two hours, is really an excuse for a series of magnificent set pieces that test Fairbanks's athletic abilities to the full. His fight in Nottingham Castle, during which he slides down a huge curtain, and his rescue of Marian—where the famous leap across the moat to the rising drawbridge occurs—are the most spectacular, but the emphasis throughout is on breathtaking action. Though the story, particularly in the rather slow first half, may be comparatively weak, many of the features and characters of the legend are present. The Merry Men—including Will Scarlett, Alan-a-Dale, Friar Tuck, and Little John—are much in evidence, though they are not introduced in the ballad tradition, and King Richard's return to England is as a disguised knight. He rescues Robin at the last moment from a hail of arrows in Nottingham Castle before the Merry Men rush in and save the day.

A score was prepared by Victor Schertzinger that made extensive use of Reginald de Koven's operetta *Robin Hood*, music that would play an indirect part in the musical design of *The Adventures of Robin Hood*.

Warner Bros. and Robin Hood

Warner Bros. had scored a huge hit with the Flynn-de Havilland pairing in *Captain Blood*, yet it was the prestige production of 1935, *A Midsummer Night's Dream*, that provided the immediate impetus for considering another Robin Hood film. Dwight Franklin in a memo to Jack Warner thought that James Cagney, who had played Bottom in *A Midsummer Night's Dream*, would "make a swell Robin Hood."[7] Warner evidently agreed, and in August 1935 Rowland Leigh was asked to work out an initial treatment of the story, with the film to be a vehicle for Cagney, and the Merry Men to be played by the studio's contract players.

Leigh worked with the studio's executive story editor, Walter MacEwen, and the research department, and by April 1936 the first forty pages were handed to executive producer Hal B. Wallis. Meanwhile, Cagney had walked out in a contractual dispute and was not to return to Warner Bros. for two years. The rising star of Errol Flynn ensured that it was he who was announced as Cagney's replacement as the lead.

Leigh's first draft was evidently problematic, as MacEwen's memo to Wallis reveals:

> The great difficulty is to use as much of the traditional Robin Hood stuff as possible, without having it appear episodic and disjointed, but I think Leigh is on the right track now. The language to be used was another problem; Leigh has evolved a good modification of the actual language of the period, but it may be possible to modify it still further if you feel the need. You will find a liberal use of ballads of the period throughout the script, and if you like this, the music that goes with them should help the feeling of the picture.[8]

On this last point, Wallis had to refuse: in May 1936, the studio signed an agreement with MGM stipulating that the Warner Bros. film would be a straight dramatic picture without any singing. MGM was planning to make a version of Robin Hood based on the Reginald de Koven/ Harry B. Smith operetta to star Nelson Eddy and Jeanette MacDonald. Warner Bros., through one of its music publishing holdings, owned the rights to the operetta and agreed to grant permission in exchange for some story material written by Bernard McConville that MGM had acquired from Reliance Pictures, along with another treatment by Philip Dunne.[9] In order to differentiate the products, which were both in de- velopment at the same time, MGM insisted that there should be no singing in the Warner Bros. film. In addition, Warner Bros. had to re- lease its film before 14 February 1938 to avoid any kind of clash with MGM. In the event, Warner Bros. was able to extend its deadline, and MGM's film never appeared, probably in large part due to the success of the Flynn film.

MacEwen's assessment of Leigh's ability to evolve a modification of the period language was evidently not shared by Wallis when he finally read the completed script. In a memo to producer Henry Blanke, who had been assigned to the film in June 1936, Wallis complains that the dialogue was "too poetical and too much like *Midsummer Night's Dream*."[10] Leigh had even wanted to omit the character of Maid Marian completely as she wasn't present in the earliest ballads, clearly an un- acceptable situation for a Hollywood film that would seek to emphasize her romantic pairing with Robin.

In April 1937 Wallis assigned a new writer, Norman Reilly Raine, to work on the script, giving him the newly acquired material from MGM. Raine had recently collaborated on a script for *The Life of Emile Zola*, and he produced a new draft by 7 July 1937. In his version, Robin is a Saxon freeman, rather than the yeoman of Leigh's script, and it is Will of Gamwell who appears at the banquet in Hagthorn Castle to challenge Prince John. Leigh's spectacular and climactic siege of Not- tingham Castle has been dropped, and a new opening jousting tourna- ment added, much in the manner of *Ivanhoe* and the 1922 *Robin Hood*. The latter was suggested by the film's first director, William Keighley, much to the chagrin of Raine: "The Jousting Tournament never can be anything but a prologue which, if done with the magnificence Mr. Keighley sees, will have the disastrous effect of putting the climax of the picture at the beginning."[11]

In August 1937, Seton I. Miller was assigned to help Raine with the writing so that the script could be ready by 10 September. The deci- sion to make *The Adventures of Robin Hood* in Technicolor was made as early as May 1937, and the need for specialist Technicolor equip- ment, and the presence of Natalie Kalmus as Technicolor consultant, required strict scheduling on Wallis's part. The film finally started shooting on 27 September 1937, with Raine in attendance to revise the script, now jointly authored by himself and Miller.

The troublesome end to the film was finally worked out satisfactorily. The original storming of Nottingham Castle by Richard's army in Leigh's version was clearly too expensive for the cost-conscious Warner Bros., and the alternate version with a confrontation in Sherwood Forest lacked the necessary punch. With the recent coronation of George VI and the successful coronation scene in another Flynn film, *The Prince and the Pauper*, in mind, Raine proposed a coronation finale that would see Richard's army reduced to a handful of men. The jousting tournament was finally dropped and several other scenes tweaked, with comic material added for the character of Much-the-Miller's-Son (played by Herbert Munden).

Perhaps the greatest deviation from the established form of the legend found in the 1938 Warner Bros. film is the centrality afforded Sir Guy of Gisbourne and, to a lesser extent, Prince John. Admittedly, both Sir Guy and Prince John feature prominently in the Douglas Fairbanks version of Robin Hood, with Sir Guy acting as both a rival for Maid Marian and an assassin sent by John to kill Richard. Yet in the old ballads, it is the Sheriff of Nottingham who is Robin's chief opponent; Sir Guy is merely a medieval hit man hired by the sheriff to hunt him down. Prince John, though found scheming against King Richard in *Ivanhoe* and *Maid Marian*, is nowhere to be seen in Ritson's anthology of sources; nor is he found in Pyle's 1893 book. Indeed, both Ritson and Pyle set much of their Robin Hood story in the time of Henry II. Warner Bros. needed an effective foil to Errol Flynn's Robin, however, and opted for the cunning intelligence of Basil Rathbone as Sir Guy and an effete, yet menacing, Claude Rains as Prince John. The Sheriff of Nottingham, as played by Melville Cooper, is reduced to a bumbling buffoon, though the idea of the archery tournament as a trap to capture Robin remains his idea. Robin's Merry Men are all played by established character actors, with Eugene Pallette's Friar Tuck turning in a star performance. Alan Hale reprised his 1922 role as Little John, while the part of Will Scarlett—originally to be played by Flynn's great friend David Niven—was given to Patric Knowles.

The initial shooting was done on location, with Chico's Bidwell Park, some 350 miles north of Los Angeles, serving as Sherwood Forest. Almost immediately there were signs that the director, William Keighley (who had worked with Flynn on *The Prince and the Pauper* in 1937), was falling behind schedule. A second unit director, B.

Reeves "Breezy" Eason, was dispatched to speed things up. Olivia de Havilland arrived on 22 October to film her scenes (until 16 September, it was to have been Anita Louise to play the part of Maid Marian) and filming finally finished in Chico on 8 November, some nine days behind schedule. The company returned to Los Angeles and, in mid-November, filmed the central archery tournament at Busch Gardens in Pasadena. By 30 November, now fifteen days behind schedule and over budget, Wallis acted: Keighley was replaced by the Hungarian-born director Michael Curtiz, who also brought along his favorite cameraman, Sol Polito, to replace Tony Gaudio. The company shot the film's interior scenes at Warner's Burbank studios, and a few exterior scenes on the back lot; the exterior portcullis/Nottingham gate set was located on the Warner Bros. ranch in Calabasas.

Despite Curtiz's more efficient methods, though, the production continued to lag behind schedule, prompting Wallis to send a memo to Tenny Wright on 11 January: "It looks to me as though you and your department have no control over the making of the pictures at all any more. It seems that a director is permitted to go out and do anything he pleases."[12] William Dieterle was brought in to direct a montage sequence featuring Crippen the Arrowmaker, and by the time the film finished shooting at 3:10 a.m. on 15 January 1938, it was considerably over budget. When an additional shooting day was required a week later, it put the production thirty-eight days behind schedule, at a cost of $1,900,000 (the 28 September budget had been $1,440,000).[13] For a cost-conscious studio like Warner Bros., this was unheard of. Indeed, Jack Warner's need to save money often resulted in walks around the studio lot, turning off light switches left on unnecessarily and checking that everyone was working as they should be. As *Fortune* magazine reported, this could have the most unfortunate result for some employees:

> On one such trip he heard the new gateman singing Verdi arias in a beautiful voice. Engaging him in talk he learned that the man was indeed a serious student of voice and practiced daily. "Which would you rather be," asked Jack, "a singer or a gateman?" The man, all warm inside, said "Oh, a singer." "You're fired," said Jack simply.[14]

As will be discussed in chapter 4, Korngold was given eight weeks, from 12 February to 3 April, to complete the composition and recording of the score. Following the film's postproduction, and at least one private showing to Gradwell Sears on 1 April, after which he called *The Adventures of Robin Hood* "unquestionably the perfection of mass entertainment,"[15] the film sneak-previewed in Pomona on 7 April,[16] prompting Wallis to claim, "In history of our company never have we had picture that scored in front of audience like this did."[17] A second sneak preview followed on 11 April at the Warner Bros. downtown theater in Los Angeles, after which Hal Wallis wired S. Charles Einfeld (director of advertising and publicity) to say:

> EXPECT HAVE OPEN PREVIEW ROBIN HOOD END THIS WEEK OR FIRST NEXT WEEK STOP HAD SECOND SNEAK PREVIEW WARNER BROTHERS DOWNTOWN THEATER AND WENT EVEN BETTER THAN AT POMONA WHICH IS HARD TO BELIEVE STOP[18]

On Monday, 18 April, at 8:20 p.m., an open preview of the film was held at the Warner Bros. Hollywood Theater, while a second followed a week later. Invited guests to the 25 April open preview included Max Reinhardt and director Ernst Lubitsch. Warner Bros. received numerous cables and letters of congratulation in the following days, with Rufus LeMaire from RKO adding that the "musical score was superb" as a postscript to his 27 April letter.[19]

The picture premièred on 12 May, prompting Frank Nugent to comment in the next day's *New York Times* that the film was "a richly produced, bravely bedecked, romantic and colorful show, it leaps boldly to the forefront of this year's best and can be calculated to rejoice the eights, rejuvenate the eighties and delight those in between."[20] *Variety* called it "cinematic pageantry at its best," though Mark Van Doren in *The Nation* suggested it was over-polished and "too clean."[21] It seems clear, though, that the film was a huge success, prompting a theatrical re-release ten years later. It continued to maintain its popularity on television.

Genre of the Swashbuckler

Before examining various critical readings of *The Adventures of Robin Hood*, it would be appropriate to consider the film's place within the narrative traditions of the Hollywood genre film. The aesthetic and cultural value of genre films, and the action-adventure film in particular, has long been debated in film studies. Yvonne Tasker, for example, points out that the action-adventure film has been traditionally deemed "noisy and brash, judged empty at best and politically reactionary at worst."[22] Yet recent years have seen a revival in scholarly interest,[23] with much of this work concerned with decoding the ideological significance of action cinema, particularly with respect to gender. Genre criticism as a whole has also only relatively recently been seen as an appropriate approach to take to Hollywood film of the studio era. Indeed, as Tom Ryall points out, in confronting "aspects of popular film—conventionality, formulas, stars, industrial production systems, publicity—which jarred with conventional approaches to artistic production and were often overlooked by auteur critics," the first wave of genre criticism in the 1970s moved beyond individuality to embrace commonality.[24]

As Thomas Schatz argued in 1981, though, traditional studies of the genre film tended to treat it as an isolated system of conventions and paid scant attention to the role of the audience and the production system in maintaining these common elements.[25] While non-genre films may have attracted greater critical attention, it was the genre films that constituted the vast majority of box office successes during the studio era. This relationship is evidently self-perpetuating: success inspires repetition, leading to a degree of uniformity and the establishment of certain conventions.

Schatz outlined a broad distinction between genres of determinate space and those of indeterminate space—between genres of an ideologically contested setting and those of an ideologically stable setting, respectively. The genres of determinate space, such as the Western or gangster films, situate their action in a cultural realm in which fundamental values are in a state of sustained conflict; in contrast, the genres of indeterminate space, like the musical or the screwball comedy, often involve romantic couples inhabiting a civilized, stable space. Schatz argued that the determinate space genres uphold values of social order, and it will become clear that *The Adventures of Robin Hood*, as a swashbuckler, supports this.

The swashbuckler is, in Brian Taves's formulation, a subgenre of the historical adventure movie, and its most recognizable type.

> This form usually opens with oppression imposed on a peaceful land, resulting in a rebellion that...calls forth a leader dedicated to the rights of the people...With the hero's aid, at the conclusion of the swashbuckling adventure either a just regime is restored or a new, improved establishment is created, replacing one liable to transgression by tyrants.[26]

The swashbuckler also places greater emphasis on the individual than other adventure stories, often ending with a duel "in which the hero single-handedly kills the principal villain."[27] This is certainly the case in *The Adventures of Robin Hood*; indeed, as Taves points out, the Robin Hood myth is the prototype of the swashbuckler.[28] The reliance on character types, and a stock cast of character actors, also allows for numerous intertextual references between these films. Alan Hale, for example, played the character of Little John on three separate occasions[29] and often played a similar role in support of Errol Flynn's hero (in *The Sea Hawk*, *Dodge City*, and *The Adventures of Don Juan*). As will be discussed in the final section of this chapter, the legacy of the swashbuckler genre still continues today, and, as part of the swash-buckler Text, *The Adventures of Robin Hood* played a significant role.

Reading *Robin Hood*

Although *The Adventures of Robin Hood* is sometimes included in crit-ics' lists of 'greatest films,'[30] there is surprisingly little attention paid to it in the academic literature of film studies. Perhaps dismissed as mere popcorn genre entertainment, though admittedly of a superior kind, few have examined it closely or tried to unpick the meanings encoded within its Text. Taves has argued that the swashbuckler is the most formulaic of adventure forms,[31] and this has perhaps dissuaded critical attention. Possibly this is a hangover from the *auteurist* criticism of early film studies; certainly, *The Adventures of Robin Hood* could not be described in any way as *auteurist*, if indeed any film truly can in light of poststructuralist philosophy's impact on the discipline. On the contrary, *Robin Hood* is commonly lauded as a supreme example of the collaborative studio system working at its peak.[32] This attitude no doubt discouraged *auteurist* critics like Andrew Sarris from addressing the film; if authorial agency could not be identified, neither could a com-municable message. Similarly the film's status as a 'formulaic genre film' would suggest that it has nothing significant to say. Yet with the rise of poststructuralism in French theory and the application of Der-rida, Foucault, and others to the cinema, films became texts that could be read like any other; they required no controlling *auteur* to close off meaning in a logocentric way, instead opening up a plurality of inter-pretative possibilities.

While authorship discourses have recently been the subject for several books that argue for a reevaluation of authorial agency, espe-cially among minority groups,[33] the poststructuralist agenda has at least opened the door for an examination of studio-era films that exemplify what Bazin called "the genius of the system."[34] *The Adventures of Robin Hood* is certainly one of them, and yet few have examined it as a social document of its time or attempted to read the more complex meanings beneath its apparently simplistic or formulaic surface. Ina Rae Hark's article "The Visual Politics of *The Adventures of Robin Hood*" from 1976 is one such attempt.[35] Though Hark emphasizes the way in which Robin's vitality, as reflected in the camera movement, disrupts the static, geometrical, and inflexible pattern of the Normans, this serves a broader point that highlights the various ways in which the film addresses the relationship of the individual to government; how the action of the film is dominated by the efforts of a charismatic individual to restore responsible government and economic stability to his country; and how, in large part, the characters of Richard and Robin stand for the figure of Franklin D. Roosevelt. Thus the film encompasses the dual concerns of America in the late 1930s as a country in a transitional period between the Depression and the threat of war in Europe and the Pacific. *Robin Hood* can be read, then, as both a retrospective look at Roosevelt's New Deal democracy and, in light of the studio's antifascist attitudes, a warning to America of the coming struggle against Germany. This latter point, of course, has special resonance for Korngold as an Austrian Jew who, as we have seen, owed his involvement in the film to Hitler's Anschluss in Austria.

Warner Bros. and the New Deal

> In their formulaic narrative process, genre films celebrate the most fundamentally ideological precepts—they examine and affirm "Americanism" with all its rampant conflicts, contradictions, and ambiguities.[36]

The American film industry in the 1930s was heavily affected by the Depression following the 1929 Wall Street crash, and Warner Bros. was no exception. The company saw a drop in profits of $28.5 million between 1929 and 1933, but gradually recovered in line with Roosevelt's National Recovery Administration (NRA).[37] As Nick Roddick has argued, however, the kinds of films made by Warner Bros., and other studios, in the 1930s were strongly influenced by the prevailing economic and organizational circumstances: an economy of production method necessarily lead to an economy of narrative method.[38] Thus the strong genre demarcations in place throughout this period, and indeed the very existence of films like *The Adventures of Robin Hood*, owe much to the nation's economic situation.

Roosevelt's New Deal and his NRA gradually brought the country back to economic health, yet his solutions were not particularly radical. As Roddick argues, they stressed individual initiative with the incentives of personal and family prosperity: "America would be saved by restoring not revolutionising her economic base. Redistribution of wealth on a large scale and a radical change of direction were not part of the programme."[39]

Warner Bros., as a studio, was directly influenced by Roosevelt's New Deal. Both Harry and Jack Warner were strong admirers and advocates of Roosevelt's policies, and Roosevelt rewarded Jack's loyalty by naming him Los Angeles chairman of the NRA. In 1933 the studio even produced a one-reel musical promotion for the NRA called *The Road Is Open Again*, starring Dick Powell as a songwriter who falls asleep while writing a song about the NRA; he dreams of former presidents appearing and assuring him that Roosevelt is the way forward. Though Harry withdrew his support in 1934–1935 in response to his indictment for antitrust violations, along with executives from Paramount and RKO,[40] Roddick has argued that the themes of Warner's films throughout the 1930s reflect the social progress of the country. They parallel the journey from "severe depression to recovery, growth, complacency and finally into a new crisis as the economic isolationism on which the New Deal's successes had been built came into conflict with the principle of morality which had been its official ideology."[41] More than this, the films also contain many of the ideological features of Roosevelt's first two terms of office, and many of the same contradictions. *The Adventures of Robin Hood* is a particularly good example of this point.

The film seems to be concerned with the restoration of good government, represented by King Richard, and an accompanying economic stability. In earlier drafts of the script, as Roddick points out, Robin was a yeoman; the change to a noble outlaw is clearly a conservative move that chimes with the New Deal's emphasis on personal and family prosperity. At the conclusion of the film, Robin is rewarded with the restoration of his land, and Richard pardons the men of Sherwood. Although promising to "banish all injustices" from his land, Richard promises no sweeping revolution; it is a conservative restoration of an economic stability perceived to be just, even if does not promise equality, that is the aim of Robin and Richard. Few can doubt that Robin, with a wife and a family, would maintain his contacts with the Merry Men. Even within Robin's band, there is little equality: during the banquet scene in Sherwood Forest, the poorer members of his supporters are left in the shadows to be the object of fascination for Marian and the catalyst for her conversion to Robin's way of thinking, while the upper echelons of the Merry Men feast in sunlight wearing bright Norman robes.

Robin's attack on the Normans' behavior sometimes seems to reflect criticism of their economic policy rather than outrage at their treatment of the Saxons. Thus, when he appears at the banquet at Nottingham castle, he admonishes Sir Guy of Gisbourne for not feeding his servants, remarking that they'd "work better" were he to do so. It is clear, too, that Prince John's schemes are structured around money. His method of oppression, though also manifested with the ear-loppings and eye-gougings about which the Saxons complain, is primarily economic. His punishment of the Saxons, though, as he himself remarks jokingly, is clearly unsustainable: "Else we'll have nobody left to till our land or pay the tax." Even his method of reward is based on land: he offers Dickon, a disgraced knight, a return to rank and "the manor and estate of Robin of Locksley" as reward for the murder of Richard. Robin's resistance to John could thus be read as an admonishment of poor economics. Even Robin's supposed policy of robbing from the rich and giving to the poor doesn't always ring true. After capturing Sir Guy's treasure caravan, Marian skeptically asks if Robin will keep the loot for himself; he asks his men and they reply: "Hold it for Richard! It belongs to the King!" Nowhere is there the suggestion that it should be divided among the poor. Similarly when King Richard, disguised as an abbot, is intercepted by Robin and his men, he is allowed to retain half of his money merely by claiming to be a friend of Richard. It is clear, then, that Robin is not a revolutionary, but as Hark argues, a counterrevolutionary, determined to restore responsible government and sensible economic policy and maintain the social status quo that keeps disgraced knights in their place.

As Roddick notes, however, the American economic isolationism that allowed the New Deal to prove so successful faced a moral dilemma with the rise of the European dictators in the late 1930s. *The Adventures of Robin Hood* also encapsulates this dilemma, as Robin remarks to the disguised Richard that he'd condemn anything, including Holy crusades, that left the task of holding England to outlaws like him. The economic problems of England (read: America), the film seems to say, can be solved only at the cost of international isolationism; as in *Ivanhoe*, social stability seems to come at a moral price. Thus even a great moral crusade, like ridding Europe of fascism, should come second to domestic stability. This, of course, comes into conflict with the other clear reading of the film that stresses the importance, shared by Roosevelt and Warner Bros., of standing up to oppression, namely, Nazi tyranny, of which more below. Thus the very contradictions and dilemmas that characterize Roosevelt's domestic and foreign policies are encapsulated in the figures of Richard and Robin. Richard, though he admits that he "ought never to have left England" is the crusading version of Roosevelt, determined to fight in foreign lands for a noble cause; Robin, in some ways, represents the isolationist policies of the New Deal, determined to restore economic stability and yet also willing to fight against oppression to achieve this. An America recovered from the Depression faced just these dilemmas in the late 1930s.

Warner Bros. and Antifascism

Warner Bros. was one of the first Hollywood studios to recognize the growing threat of Hitler and to employ an overtly anti-Nazi policy, in pictures like *Confessions of a Nazi Spy* (1939). Michael Birdwell characterizes this as a "crusade" to alert Americans to the growing menace of Nazism and fascism, at home and abroad, and ascribes the majority of credit to Harry Warner, the devout Jew and president of the company, rather than to Jack, his playboy brother in charge of production.[42] Harry, it seems, recognized the danger early; while he had considered buying Germany's UFA film studio, he changed his mind after a trip to the country in 1932. Germany constituted a major share of the European market, but Warner Bros. refused to have anything to do with the country altogether after 1934, in stark contrast to the other Hollywood majors who, despite being headed by Jewish immigrants, continued to show their films in Nazi Germany until 1940. Warner Bros. raised money for displaced Jews (Jack sponsored a dinner for Thomas Mann in 1938) and supported the United Jewish Appeal; in 1936 Harry donated free airtime on the radio network KFWB to the Anti-Nazi League. Moreover, the company continued its campaign against Nazism despite continued criticism from isolationists, nascent fascist organizations in the United States, and the Production Code Administration (PCA), headed by the anti-Semitic Joseph Breen. Though no explicitly anti-Nazi film was produced until 1938 (the animated *Bosko's Picture Show*) due to the restrictions imposed by the Motion Pictures Producers and Distributors Association (MPPDA), the PCA, and the State Department, the studio turned to headlines at home and historical allegory to expose the danger. In the former category, the studio produced *Black Legion*, based on the group active in Detroit that

had grown out of the Ku Klux Klan of the 1920s and was responsible
for fifty-seven murders or attempted murders over a six-year period. In
the latter category, the studio produced a number of prestige biopics
and costume dramas, including *The Life of Emile Zola* (1937), which
exposed the anti-Semitism in the French military, and *Juarez* (1939),
which Birdwell sees as an appeal to Mexico and Latin America to help
see off Nazism.[43]

Warner Bros. films also actively preached interventionism. Both
Jack and Harry Warner were staunch supporters of the British cause
and believed that America's security was linked to Britain's. Films like
The Dawn Patrol (1938) portrayed the courage of British pilots, and the
historical allegory of England under threat from the Spanish Armada in
The Sea Hawk (1940) could not have failed to be noticed while American newsreels shown before the picture carried pictures from the Battle
of Britain. The studio's most blatant appeal for intervention can perhaps be seen in *Sergeant York* (1941), the story of a pacifist who recognizes the need to fight to maintain his country's freedoms, while
other films—such as *The Fighting 69th* (1940)—could be construed as
carrying a more conflicted message that tried to balance isolationists
and interventionists.[44]

The Adventures of Robin Hood can be read in the light of this anti-
Nazi policy as evincing a belligerent policy of non-appeasement; Birdwell goes so far as to call it an explicitly "antifascist film."[45] Robin and
his men, through their oath to fight to the death against their Norman
oppressors, begin a guerrilla campaign of resistance, much as the un-
derground movements in occupied Europe would do in reality just a
few years later.[46] The element of racial intolerance and oppression visited upon the Saxons by the Normans also chimes with contemporaneous events, though the notion of a Norman-Saxon conflict at this time
has little basis in historical fact. Robin, in contrast, claims to hate injustice, not the Normans. Even the collaboration of the Bishop of the
Black Canons with Prince John and Sir Guy's evil plans has certain
parallels with the perceived complicity of the Catholic church in fan-
ning the flames of Austrian anti-Semitism;[47] the rather low church represented by the beer-drinking Friar Tuck, on the other hand, is firmly
allied with Robin's cause.

This, of course, had added resonance for Korngold, as an Austrian
Jew whose property had been confiscated by the Nazis and whose
country was in the hands of a foreign aggressor. As with the socially
unstable England of 1819 and the country portrayed in *Ivanhoe*, the
parallels between the England of the film and the Austria of 1938 could

not be clearer. Even Chancellor Schuschnigg, as a Catholic, could perhaps be found mirrored in the high church practices of the Bishop of
the Black Canons, unwilling or unable to prevent the growing power of
Prince John/Hitler, though this figure could also be read as a veiled
attack on Father Charles Caughlin, a noted fascist sympathizer in
America. Though the Anschluss in Austria had not yet taken place by
the time filming completed, the movie appears to have special resonance with contemporary events; even the first spoken line of the
film—"News has come from Vienna"—seems strangely apt. Indeed,
the score may have done much to fuel these comparisons; it was jokingly referred to as "Robin Hood in the Vienna Woods" by members of
the Warner Bros. orchestra, and Korngold could not have failed to see
the connection when using "Miß Austria" as one of the score's main
themes. Adding an Austrian cultural flavor to the film's evocation of a
mythic England was perhaps the only way that Korngold could fight
back against the tide of contemporary politics. Robin's love for his
country is also explicitly linked with his growing love for Marian, and
it is her feelings for him that prompt her own act of rebellion against
her Norman kin. As I will argue in chapter 5, the score plays a large
part in linking these two narrative threads.

Other Readings

In recognizing the characters of Much and Bess as comic reflections of
Robin and Marian, it is possible to investigate the film as a social text
that comments on the nature of class; in their shared status of outlaws, a
certain amount of social equality allows Robin, a nobleman, to mix
with a serf like Much, while still maintaining something of the hierarchy of a master-servant relationship. Much and Bess, played by Herbert
Munden and Una O'Connor, were certainly not the matinee idols that
Errol Flynn and Olivia de Havilland were, and this visual contrast between the two couples seems to accentuate the incongruity of their
similar situations and, therefore, to reinforce the notion of a social up-
heaval. With the restoration of the status quo at the end of the film, the
social roles of the four lovers, one feels, are likewise restored.

Throughout the film, there is a conflict between Man and Nature,
with the Normans portrayed as violators of the natural world: they are
associated with the town and seem threatened by the countryside; their
clothes are bright and not easily camouflaged; and they are forced to
travel in convoy through Sherwood as if it is enemy territory. To see
the Normans on horseback suggests their attempts to subjugate nature.

Robin, on the other hand, is associated with the countryside and is a defender of 'England'; he and his men wear earth colors and jump out of trees, and he will gladly spend a night out in the open, extolling the virtues of such a lifestyle to Will Scarlett. In contrast to the Normans, then, Robin on a horse is suggestive of Man and Nature working in harmony, organically. As Ina Rae Hark notes:

> Robin and his men are portrayed in natural surroundings and are characterized by spontaneity of action and unrestrained motion...They also possess an enormous sense of fun concerning life and themselves...The Normans lack this sense of fun altogether...In contrast to the men of Sherwood, they are rigid and artificial.[48]

Richard, the true monarch, also belongs to the natural world in the same way as Robin, traveling through Sherwood and revealing his sovereignty in the woods rather than proclaiming it from Nottingham Castle. Similarly, the original end shot of the film, of Robin and Marian riding off on horseback through the countryside, makes the association of the natural world and the heroes of the film even stronger. That the film actually finishes with the closing of the castle door sends Robin and Marian into a mythical and idealized natural world, closing the door on the symbol of Norman oppression, the castle. That we, as spectators, are left on the inside, bolted into the hard stone world of civilized man, is surely felt as a lack alleviated only by the resolution offered by the score's conclusive cadence. Given that the film could be read as encoding mythic England as a nostalgic view of contemporary Austria, with the Viennese love of the woods and public gardens, this love of nature that the film seems to propound is particularly appropriate.

The film can also be potentially read from a gendered point of view. Robin's masculinity is constantly threatened, both implicitly by Sir Guy as a rival for Marian, and overtly by Little John who, upon being threatened by a longbow when he only has a staff, asks "aren't you man enough to...." Robin cuts him off before he can finish his question, slighted by the questioning of his masculinity. In fact, Robin's frequent acts of aggression against Sir Guy, the Sheriff, and even his own men could be read as a manifestation of the kinds of sexual violence discussed by Lawrence Kramer in his book *After the Lovedeath*. Kramer offers a convincing explanation for the punishment of femininity found at all levels of culture, though his approach has been criticized for its moralizing tone.[49] This Kramer does by invoking the notion of gender polarity:

Gender polarity is set in motion when a man's behavior meets (or a woman's accepts or encourages) most or all of three conditions. First, the man claims to occupy the masculine subject position absolutely rather than relatively: to occupy it, so to speak, as the lender rather than the borrower of the phallus. Second, the "claimer" (Freud's term for a phallic woman, but here referring to men acting as such phallic women are imagined to act) embodies his status as a "borrower" in the person of someone else, someone who, as a woman (or effeminate man) is not even entitled to borrow. Third, the claimer consolidates, in the person of the false, feminine, "borrower", a positive form of his actual lack of entitlement, which he identifies with her femininity...Even the slightest fault line in idealization or desire can provoke contempt or aggression in excess of any apparent reason.[50]

Robin's ultimate target is Prince John, played in an effete way by Claude Rains, surely the effeminate man considered disentitled to claim the masculine subject position. Similarly, the Sheriff of Nottingham is characterized as cowardly and feminized (while Sir Guy rushes off to fight at the close of the film, the Sheriff cannot unsheathe his sword and rushes off to hide). Only Sir Guy of Gisbourne matches Robin's perceived masculinity. Indeed Sir Guy also questions the Sheriff's courage and intelligence, noting that "you couldn't capture him [Robin] if he sat in your lap shooting arrows at a crow." While Robin consents to take a slap from Sir Guy after being captured—and Antonia Quirke has argued that a slap in the cinema is sexual[51]—he refuses to suffer such an indignity from the Sheriff, kicking him in the chest instead.

When Sir Guy has been dispatched, though, the fight seems to go out of Robin; he allows his men to deal with the remaining soldiers while he goes off to rescue Marian, threatening the guard with a bent sword in preference to killing him. Robin's masculinity is thus defined both through his punishment of the false borrowers (the Sheriff and Prince John) and through his rivalry with his equal (Sir Guy). Once Sir Guy is dead, with no perceived rival to the masculine subject position, and the effeminate men captured, his sexual violence can end.

The Robin Hood Legacy

The Adventures of Robin Hood's success inspired other Flynn swashbucklers at Warner Bros., including *The Sea Hawk* (1940) and, much later, *The Adventures of Don Juan* (1948), thus resulting in a certain degree of type-casting for the actor. At a wider generic level, too, the adventure film has also continued to exert a sizable influence on Hollywood's output. Though Brian Taves points out that the period of the adventure genre's principal popularity coincided with the golden age of the Hollywood studio system, he discusses films of the 1970s and 1980s that began a new cycle of adventure films that moved toward parody, such as *The Three Musketeers* (1973), *The Count of Monte Cristo* (1974), and *Robin and Marian* (1976).[52] Moreover, Steve Neale saw the success of *Robin Hood: Prince of Thieves* (1991) initiating the latest cycle of adventure films,[53] something that Taves also recognized in that film's return to a more classical form. This 'fifth' cycle, Neale argues, includes *1492: Conquest of Paradise* (1992), *Rob Roy* (1995), and *Braveheart* (1995). Similarly, more recent films like *The Mask of Zorro* (1998), *The Count of Monte Cristo* (2001), and *Pirates of the Caribbean: The Curse of the Black Pearl* (2003)—with Johnny Depp's Captain Jack Sparrow a shadowy reflection of the witty Errol Flynn stereotype—demonstrate that the adventure film still has currency.

Notably, though, Keira Knightley's role in *Pirates of the Caribbean* points to the changing attitude to gender evinced in the contemporary adventure film. Though Neale notes that there is nothing inherent in the structure of the genre to specify the gender of its protagonists,[54] and discusses the female-centered adventure films of the 1910s and the female Westerns of the 1920s, there is certainly a gender bias toward male heroics in pre-World War II cinema. In that sense, *The Adventures of Robin Hood* stands near a crossroads. The impact of war on Hollywood would ensure that the departure of male stars allowed for the reappearance of the female lead, and *The Adventures of Robin Hood* can be seen in the light of this growing power of women within Hollywood. Though Olivia de Havilland was herself a leading figure in campaigning for actors' rights within the studio system, the strong roles for women seen in *Jezebel* (1938), *Gone with the Wind* (1939), and *Mrs. Miniver* (1942) are perhaps all the more notable when contrasted with the rather supporting nature of Maid Marian in *The Adventures of Robin Hood*. Though de Havilland's character, along with Una O'Connor's Bess, has markedly more impact on the narrative than in the 1922 *Robin Hood*, the film is, in part, a farewell to the gender inequality that had dominated the adventure film. Once the war arrived, adventure movies themselves also temporarily disappeared, adding to the sense of nostalgia that the film retrospectively evokes. As will be seen in chapters 4 and 5, the score plays an important role in contributing to this nostalgic atmosphere.

4

COMPOSING *ROBIN HOOD*

The act of 'composing' a film score in the late 1930s was not as straightforward as one might imagine. In the case of *The Adventures of Robin Hood*, the composition process was so complex that it can be said to extend back some twenty years prior to the film's release and to encompass numerous authorial contributions. Similarly the different manifestations of the film score sanctioned at various points by Warner Bros., or Korngold himself, resist the notion of a unitary aesthetic object that we can label as 'the score' to *The Adventures of Robin Hood*. The score thus has a particularly wide cultural footprint that deserves extensive examination. This overview of the film's musical material will use archival evidence to chart the score's progress through pre- and post-production, and its engagement with other authorial agencies. It will examine the various extant manuscript sources and discuss Korngold's use of preexisting musical material from earlier concert and dramatic works.

Obviously, given the difficulty in identifying the 'score,' what I choose to examine inevitably highlights the analyst's role in constructing this postmodern Text. While delving into manuscript sources might seem a traditional, objective, musicological task, it is arguably anything but. The analyst of this musicological data may influence the identity of this postmodern Text as much as a reader affects its meaning and must therefore figure as yet another voice to be considered in the weave of musical fabric.

Preproduction

Correspondence held at the Warner Bros. archives indicates that the musical design of the film was considered as early as August 1937, a full month before principal photography began. It appears that the studio's research department was charged with locating suitable period music that could be incorporated into the film, and it is in a memo of 11 August to William Keighley that first mention of the old English tune "Summer Is Icumen In," whistled by Little John in cue 3B, is made:

> One song of the period, or to be exact, composed in 1225 has been preserved and we have the music and the words. It is evidently well known and while the words of our copy are in Old English the music is decipherable and there are instructions that will make it possible for it to be played. The title is "Summer is icumen in."[1]

The following month, Leo Forbstein produced a more extensive list of songs taken from Adam de la Halle's *The Play of Robin and Marian*, E. Duncan's *The Minstrelsy of England*, and Stanford's *The National Song Book* for possible inclusion in the film. These included "Trairiri," "Shepherdess Slender," "Ye Morrises," "Arthur a Bland," "The Barley Mow," "The Old Ewe with One Horn," "Ye Belles and Ye Flirts," "The Bailiff's Daughter of Islington," "Barbara Allen," and, once again, "Summer Is Icumen In." In addition, the studio took down the music and lyrics of two further songs, "The Old Sow" and "My Jenny," from an old Englishman who Forbstein indicated would be singing them in the picture. Evidently "The Old Sow" proved problematic with the lawyers since Rudy Vallee had recently rewritten the lyrics and many were under the impression that it was a current popular song; no trace of "My Jenny" could be found and Victor Blau was therefore "afraid to okay the number," presumably in case there was a copyright claim. The other songs, with the exception of "Trairiri" and "Shepherdess Slender," were in the public domain and could be used without fear of copyright problems. One song seems to have been recorded as 'prescore' (see the table in the appendix), to be played on set during film for the actor/actress to mime to, though it is unclear which of the songs was chosen.

In any event, Forbstein had clearly forgotten the contractual agreement made with MGM in May 1936 stipulating that *The Adventures of Robin Hood* should contain no singing (see chapter 3). Attempts were made to appeal to MGM on this point as the music department also envisaged a boys' choir singing during the coronation scene at the film's climax. Nicholas Nayfack of MGM was firm on the matter, however, and in a letter of 15 December 1937 to Roy J. Obringer (general counsel at Warner Bros.) refused outright: "The only point of differentiation between your picture and ours, in the public mind, will be the fact that yours has no musical numbers and ours is a musical picture."[2] As a result, no singing can be heard in the film, and of the work done by the music and research departments, the only old English song heard, "Summer Is Icumen In," is whistled rather than sung by Little John.

Meanwhile, Korngold, aware that his next assignment was likely to be *The Adventures of Robin Hood*,[3] had returned to Europe in May 1937 to continue work on his fifth opera, *Die Kathrin*, due to be premièred at the Vienna State Opera in the 1937–1938 season. *Robin Hood* was not forgotten, however, and the composer spent some time in Vienna's public libraries researching the legend. From the sketches he made, it is clear that he too was interested in old English songs. A page of material in his hand, found at the Library of Congress along with other sketches for *The Adventures of Robin Hood*, bears the title "Late Sixteenth-Century Dance Tunes"; it consists of a harmonized melody and a ballad (see example 4.1). The ballad can be identified as the tenor part of "A Round of Three Country Dances in One," found in Thomas Ravenscroft's 1609 collection *Pammelia*,[4] and the harmonized melody as a version of "Robin Hood and the Stranger" from Cambridge University MS D.d.9.33 fol. 81ᵛ.[5] It seems, though, that Korngold copied both musical examples directly from a single page of a secondary text, William Chappell's *Old English Music*.[6] The page in question bears the title *Robin Hood* and is part of a chapter entitled "Dance Tunes" and a subchapter with the heading "Later Sixteenth Century Dance Tunes." There seems little doubt that Chappell's book was the source of this sketch. While Korngold did not use either of these melodies in the score, they bear a distinct rhythmic and syntactical resemblance to the theme he used for Maid Marian (example 4.2). Interestingly, the chapter from which Korngold appears to have copied these melodies also mentions "Summer Is Icumen In" in its first paragraph.[7] While no evidence exists to suggest that Korngold took note of this, it is possible that the impetus to use the tune can be traced, in part, to Chappell's book. Perhaps Forbstein made the suggestion as a result of the music department's endeavors and it chimed with Korngold's own research.

Example 4.1. Late Sixteenth-Century Dance Tunes Sketch

Example 4.2. Marian's Theme (Taken from Cue 1E, Figure 9)

Postproduction

The Adventures of Robin Hood finished shooting officially on 15 January 1938, though as the production had gone vastly over time and budget, it is unsurprising that an extra day was required a week later. As executive producer Hal B. Wallis continued to edit the picture, thought was given to the film's scoring. Clearly, in light of the copyright problems encountered in preproduction, the nondiegetic score would have to carry the musical content of the film, and it is therefore unsurprising that Wallis and Henry Blanke pursued Korngold so assiduously, despite the latter's initial reluctance on first viewing the film. Indeed, the circumstances surrounding Korngold's acceptance of this job seem particularly unusual. The myth of Korngold as a composer with complete carte blanche is commonly contrasted with someone like Max Steiner, whose contract rarely allowed him to pick and choose projects, ensuring that he wrote four times as many scores as Korngold in the same period.[8] At first glance, Korngold's attitude to *Robin Hood* seems to exemplify this level of choice. Though he went as far as completing some preparatory work on the film before it finished shooting, he was still able to refuse the job once he saw the rough cut, citing the incredible amount of action as the reason (see below). This refusal, though, does not appear to have been taken seriously by the studio. Nor, perhaps, are Korngold's reasons for changing his mind as clear-cut as the myths might suggest.

On 21 January Wallis and Blanke cabled Korngold in Vienna requesting he return to Hollywood. Korngold indicated his compliance the following day, and on 24 January Wallis, evidently confident of the composer's acceptance of the job, asked for the old music card for the film's titles sequence to be removed and Korngold's credit inserted. The contents of the old music card are unknown. Blanke also wrote to Jacob Wilk (a studio story editor) in New York informing him of Korngold's plans to leave Europe aboard the *Normandie* on 29 January. He asked that someone meet him on arrival in New York and pass on the copy of the script that Blanke was mailing to Wilk.

Example 4.3. Love Theme Sketch

Korngold, along with his wife, Luzi, and their younger son, Georg, left Vienna on 25 January for Le Havre; before boarding the *Normandie*, he received a letter from his father, Dr. Julius Korngold, with the following reminder: "Don't forget my idea to use [the 1919 symphonic overture] *Sursum Corda* for the chief theme of the Captain of the Brigands!"[9] Korngold had already accepted his father's advice in earlier letters and had obtained permission from Schott to use extracts from the score. According to Brendan Carroll, Korngold had begun sketching themes while still in Vienna and continued the process on-board the ship.[10] None of the sketches, held as part of the Korngold Collection at the Library of Congress, are dated, however. These sketches include many of the principal themes and an early version of the love scene in virtually its final form (example 4.3).

Korngold arrived in New York on 3 February and—having received the copy of the script from Wilk—boarded the *Santa Fe Chief*, bound for Pasadena, the following day. On 7 February, the Korngold family arrived in California and settled in, while Wallis continued to edit the picture. On 11 February Korngold attended a screening of the film and, according to reports,[11] grew increasingly worried as the movie unfolded before him; upon its completion, he wrote a carefully worded letter of rejection to Wallis:

February 11 1938

Dear Mr Wallis

I am sincerely sorry to have to bother you once more. I do appreciate deeply your kindness and courtesy toward me, and I am aware of the fact that you have made all concessions possible to facilitate my work.

But please believe a desperate man who has to be true to himself and to you, a man who knows what he can do and what he cannot do. Robin Hood is no picture for me. I have no relation to it and there-fore, cannot produce any music for it. I am a musician of the heart, of passions and psychology; I am not a musical illustrator for a 90% action picture. Being a conscientious person, I cannot take the responsi-bility for a job which, as I already know, would leave me artistically completely dissatisfied and which, therefore, I would have to drop even after several weeks of work on it and therefore after several weeks of salary.

Therefore, let me say "no" definitely and let me say it today when no time has been lost for you as yet, since the work print will not be ready until tomorrow. And please do not try to make me change my mind; my resolve is unshakable.

I implore you not to be angry with me and not to deprive me of your friendship. For it is I who suffers mentally and financially. I ask you to weigh the pictures for which I composed the music, such as

Midsummer Night's Dream, Captain Blood, Anthony Adverse, Prince and [the] Pauper, against the one I could not make, Robin Hood. And if during the next few weeks you should have a job for me to do, you need not cable all the way to Vienna.

> With my very best regards, I am,
> Gratefully and sincerely yours,
> Erich Wolfgang Korngold[12]

The following day, Forbstein visited the Korngold's house in Toluca Lake to try to persuade the 'unshakable' composer to change his mind. Korngold had just received word of Austrian chancellor Kurt von Schuschnigg's meeting with Hitler at Berchtesgaden and reluctantly agreed to attempt the task. As Luzi Korngold later recalled, Erich had but one proviso in taking on the project of *Robin Hood*: "He didn't want a contract. His conditions were 'work from week to week, paid from week to week.' 'If I find that it's not working out, I can give up with a clear conscience; the music I have written up until then will belong to you,' he explained."[13] On 14 February, a memo was sent by Walter MacEwen to Mr. Pease that stated "Korngold is now definitely set to do the music on 'ROBIN HOOD.'"

The extent to which Korngold realized the significance of the 12 February meeting between Hitler and Schuschnigg and recognized the folly of returning to an Austria under immense pressure from her German neighbor could be questioned. Korngold was notoriously reluctant to comment on politics: when asked his opinion of Hitler upon arrival in the United States to work on *A Midsummer Night's Dream*, his only comment was that he thought Mendelssohn would outlive him.[14] Even in Vienna, the desperate situation did not become clear, according to George Clare's account, until 16 February when Arthur von Syess-Inquart's first act as Austrian Minster of the Interior was to visit Berlin.[15] Korngold was somewhat more naïve than his politically astute father and yet only at the last minute did the rest of the family leave Austria before the Anschluss on 13 March. If Jews living in Vienna could not see the danger, can we really believe Korngold, isolated in Los Angeles, possessed the political clairvoyance to accurately assess the situation? Nor did the studio take his initial refusal at all seriously, in clear opposition to Korngold's views expressed in the letter. By agreeing to Korngold's demands for a get-out-clause, a clever Forbstein seems to have placated the panicked composer, knowing that he was likely to finish the job.[16] This flexibility on the studio's part seems to be just as important in securing Korngold's services as the composer's (perhaps mythical) political savvy.

With a release date of 12 May looming, Korngold and his collaborators began work in earnest, using substantial portions of *Sursum Corda* and the "Miß Austria" cue from *Rosen aus Florida* to ease the burden (see below). Throughout this period, Korngold frantically waited for news of his family in Austria and, as Friedhofer noted, the composer lost about twenty pounds "before news got to him that his mother and father and his other son were safe. It was a bad time for him."[17]

The act of composition itself involved numerous stages that proceeded in parallel; while Korngold began work on the next cue, orchestrators and copyists would complete the process with the previous one. Korngold's initial sketching of ideas and themes would be followed by a piano short score for each cue, using type- or handwritten cue sheets to help. The short score would then be passed to the orchestrators, Hugo Friedhofer and Milan Roder, who would pen the full score version of the cue before turning it over to in-house copyists to prepare the parts and the piano-conductor score. The cue would then be recorded by the Warner Bros. orchestra with Korngold conducting from the full score. Finally, any editing or retakes requiring new music would be undertaken.

The earliest substantiated date for recording part of the score was 4 March, though fully twenty-one tracks were recorded before this date, suggesting that scoring sessions began in late February. The final scheduled date of recording was Sunday, 3 April, to meet a deadline of 8 April for the first sneak previews in Pomona and downtown Los Angeles. Wallis sent the following memo to Forbstein on 31 March:

> It is important that you score the complete last reel of "ROBIN HOOD" on Sunday [3 April], and don't let any part of it ride over until Monday. We want to rush this through and have Levinson begin duping as quickly as possible, as we want this picture completed by next Friday [8 April]—a week from tomorrow, and the only way in which we can do that is by scoring the last reel on Sunday and by finishing the duping by Tuesday night.[18]

All concerned worked until midnight on the Sunday to finish the scoring of reel 12 in order to meet Wallis's deadline. The 7 April Pomona sneak preview, however, although a huge success, evidently alerted someone's attention to some passages in the music that could be improved. In all likelihood, these were Wallis's suggestions.[19] A further recording session thus took place on 11 April to make a number of changes to the score before the first open preview on 18 April. These included subtle alternative endings and beginnings to cues and, in all likelihood, a number of 'sweeteners' (overlaid tracks) added to Robin's escape from the gallows scene (8A). As Korngold himself noted in 1940, "Changes after the preview are often painful although, fortunately, I have not suffered any particularly smarting musical losses."[20]

By 13 April Roy J. Obringer (general counsel) could send a memo to C. H. Wilder (comptroller) indicating that Korngold's task was complete and that he was entitled to the unpaid balance of his "guaranteed compensation" of $12,500. Basil Rathbone, in contrast, was paid $5,000 a week, but it seems as though Wallis and Blanke's original monetary offer to Korngold was honored, despite the agreement about being paid week to week. Though Korngold's engagement with the score was to continue in some capacity until the night before the première, the 13 April date marks the point at which the dubbing of the sound track was completed.

This brief summary of the composition process belies both the collaborative nature of the act and the complexity of the changes through which the score went. In order to appreciate this complexity, it will be necessary to examine each of the sources available to us in turn. These include manuscript sources like the full score and piano short score; aural sources, such as the *Robin Hood* radio show; and one audio-visual source, the final edited print of the film. Following this description of the various contents of the sources will be a discussion of the use of the preexisting material taken from *Sursum Corda* and *Rosen aus Florida*, the resemblances to *Die Kathrin*, and the ways in which this material was adapted. Table 4.1 details the musical cues used in the film together with a description of the accompanying action for easy reference. Each cue was labeled with a number and a letter: the number referred to the reel of film; the letter referred to its place within the reel.

Table 4.1. Summary of Musical Cues and Action

Timing	Cue	Narrative action
00:00	1A	Main title.
01:50	1B	Dissolve to the interior of Nottingham Castle. Sir Guy and Prince John are introduced.
02:33	1C	The oppression of the Saxons, and the introduction of Robin Hood and Will Scarlett. Sir Guy attempts to arrest Much the Miller's Son.
04:47	1D	Robin confronts Sir Guy and rescues Much.

Table 4.1. Summary of Musical Cues and Action (continued)

Timing	Cue	Narrative action
06:18	1E	The feast in Nottingham Castle. Introduces Maid Marian.
09:30	1F	Robin enters through the castle doors with a dead deer on his shoulders.
10:03	2A	Robin approaches Prince John and throws the deer onto the table.
14:37	2B	Robin escapes from the castle.
17:06	2C	Sir Guy's men chase Robin, Will, and Much on horseback.
19:09	3A	Much rides off to spread the word of a meeting in Sherwood. The dead Normans are laid out in the castle.
20:13	3B	Robin and Will meet Little John.
22:00	3C	Robin and Little John's fight with quarterstaffs intensifies.
22:54	3D	Robin, Little John, and Will introduce themselves. Word of the meeting in Sherwood is spread.
24:54	3E	The Saxons swear an oath to fight for a free England. The oppression of the Saxons continues while Robin metes out justice with his black arrows.
27:33	3F	A black arrow is fired into Nottingham Castle. Robin and his band come across Friar Tuck sleeping.
30:17	4A	Robin forces Tuck to carry him across the stream. Robin fights Tuck.
32:14	4B	Friar Tuck becomes a member of Robin's band. Will brings news of the treasure caravan.
33:22	4C	Preparation for the attack on Sir Guy's treasure caravan, and the attack itself.
38:27	5A	Robin's men escort the captured Sir Guy and Maid Marian to their camp.
39:45	5B	Preparation for the feast.
41:11	5C	The feast is announced. Robin and Marian eat.
43:15	5D	Robin reveals the captured gold.
44:25	5E	Robin shows Marian the poor people and bids farewell.
50:26	6A	The archery tournament. Sir Guy, Prince John, and the Sheriff of Nottingham discuss their plan.
51:52	6B	The tournament starts. Robin and his men appear in disguise.
52:58	6C	Marian, Prince John, and Sir Guy converse.
53:43	6D	Robin prepares to compete and fires his first arrow.
54:27	6E	The tournament continues. Robin is recognized and the guards close in. Robin wins the archery tournament.
58:36	7A	Robin attempts to flee but is arrested.
59:40	7B	Robin is led away to his tribunal.
61:02	7C	Robin is taken to the jail. Marian wonders how she can help.
64:40	7D	Robin is led to the gallows.
67:06	8A	Robin escapes from the gallows with the help of his men.
69:08	8B	Robin visits Marian in the castle. Love is declared.

Table 4.1 Summary of Musical Cues and Action (continued)

Timing	Cue	Narrative action
81:35	9A	Marian is arrested for trying to warn King Richard of the treasonous plans of Prince John, Sir Guy, and the Bishop of the Black Canons and is brought before a tribunal.
84:11	9B	Much waits to intercept Dickon.
84:42	10A	Much and Dickon fight.
85:15	10B	A disguised King Richard rides through Sherwood and meets Robin.
86:37	10C	Richard and his men accompany Robin and his men to their camp. Will finds Much, who informs Robin of the plan against Richard.
88:46	10D	Richard reveals himself.
89:48	10E	The coronation procession to Nottingham Castle.
92:54	11A	Prince John processes to the throne. The bishop challenges Prince John. Both Richard and Robin throw off their disguises.
94:23	11B	Battle ensues.
95:33	11C	The duel between Robin and Sir Guy.
98:08	11D	Robin, having dispatched Sir Guy, races to free Marian. The battle ends.
99:48	11E	Robin asks Richard for a pardon for his men and for Marian's hand. Robin and Marian take their leave.
101:19	11F	End title.

Sketches and Cue Sheets

Korngold's initial thoughts about the music are found in the sketches, some of which are fragments of themes with labels in a mixture of English and German ("Guy" and "Duell"), while others are more extensive in nature.[21] While many of these sketches may predate Korngold's first viewing of the film, it appears as though the love scene (cue 8B) was one of the first to reach its final form, since it exists in a sketch form (an unaccompanied melody on a single stave, with a few suggested harmonies) that corresponds almost exactly with its realization in both the short and full scores (see example 4.3). Korngold was evidently concerned with the balance of the scene and even notes down the bar structure at the bottom of the second page. Lasting a total of 130 bars, he splits it into sections of 31, 29, 31, 31, and 8 bars. The only differences between the sketches and the short score are the reduction of the first section from 31 to 30 bars, as a result of a diminution of rhythm 2 before figure 3; the addition of an extra bar between figures 23 and 24;

and some slight changes between figure 17 and the bar before figure 20.

Nine cue sheets, some in the composer's hand and some typed, are extant.[22] Each gives information for a particular reel of film on shot lengths, in either seconds or feet/frames and seconds. These timings are sometimes already grouped into musical cues, as is the case with the reel 7 cue sheet (see example 4.4). Each of the four musical cues in the reel starts with the first event listed on the cue sheet; however, the cue sheet does not detail every stop and start of the music as might be expected. Rather, it seems to function as an aid to Korngold in preparing the short score.

```
                     ADVENTURES OF ROBIN HOOD

                            REEL 7

#1 -  ROBIN TRIES TO ESCAPE TO HORSES - - - -  11 Seconds
      HORSES TO ROBIN ON GROUND - - - - - -    16    "          7 + 12
      ROBIN ON GROUND TO SLAP ON FACE - - - -  19    "


#2 -  "TAKE HIM AWAY" to FADE OUT - - - - - - - 16    "
      FADE IN TO DIALOG (TRIBUNAL) - - - - - -  16    "


#3 -  END TRIBUNAL TO DISSOLVE - - - - - - -    10    "
      DISSOLVE TO PUSH - - - - - - -           10    "
      PUSH DOWN STAIRS TO CLOSEUP ON FLOOR      3     "
      CLOSEUP TO 1st HAMMERING - - - - - -     11     "
      FIRST HAMMERING TO FLOWERS - - - - -      7     "
      FLOWERS TO CLOSEUP MARION BEFORE
          SHE SAYS "BESS!" - - - - - - - - -   33     "


#4 -  FADE IN GALLOWS SEQUENCE TO END REEL - -  2 minutes 28 seconds
```

Example 4.4. Cue Sheet for Reel 7

The handwritten cue sheet for the duel in reel 11 between Robin and Sir Guy is particularly interesting, as it reveals something of the musical structure of the cue (see example 4.5). Korngold lists twenty-five separate events and divides them into three numbered sections of twenty-six, twenty-four, and sixty-seven seconds, with an introduction of fourteen seconds and concluding sections of sixteen and a half, two, and nine and a half seconds. The first fourteen seconds of both the picture and the music do seem like an introductory section before the duel proper starts. Also of note is the cue sheet for cue 8A. This was one of the cues that made extensive use of *Sursum Corda* and, as a result, Korngold does not bother to note down the events at the start of the cue that would be accompanied by the earlier existing material; rather, he starts his cue sheet at the point where new material was composed.

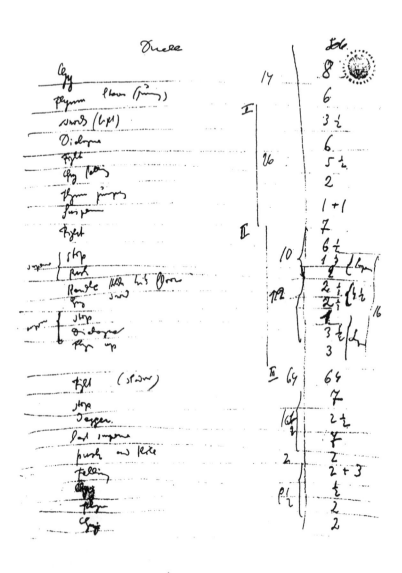

Example 4.5. Cue Sheet for 11C

Table 4.2 summarizes the content of the cue sheets.

Table 4.2. The Cue Sheets

Page	Reel	Contents	Comments
1	1	2 cues separated by a broken line: the first cue lasts 58 seconds with 11 events listed; the second lasts 1:06 with 6 events listed.	Typed in English with break-downs written by Korngold (EWK). The first cue is actually only half a cue (from figure 5 in 1C); the second is cue 1D.
2	[11]	25 separate events marked.	"Duell" handwritten (EWK). This is cue 11C. See example 4.5.
3	4	22 events listed totaling 4 minutes 28 seconds.	Typed in English with a few handwritten marks (EWK). This became cue 4C.
4	7	4 cues.	Typed in English.
5	8	7 events listed with timings in seconds and feet/frames.	Handwritten in English (EWK). This is from figure 8 in cue 8A.
6	10	5 events listed with timings in seconds and feet/frames.	Handwritten in English (virtually illegible EWK). This is 10E.
7	2	2 events lasting 13 and 11 seconds.	Handwritten in German (EWK): "Robin Hood geht zum Tisch " " spricht bis er das Reh wirft am Tisch" [Robin Hood approaches the table; Robin Hood speaks until he throws the deer on the table].
8		6 events listed.	Illegible.
9	6	"VI/E." 4 events listed lasting total of 37 seconds.	Handwritten (EWK) in English, though largely illegible.

Short Score

The extant short score, written in pencil, is an almost complete version of the score in two, three, or four staves. Though mostly in Korngold's own hand, a number of pages are written in the hand of Milan Roder, while other sections appear to have been copied out again in a neater hand by Hugo Friedhofer.

Korngold's compositional shorthand provides us with some initial clues to the order of the score's composition. For the most part, these

Table 4.3. The Short Score

Cue	Hand[23]	Title	Comments
1A	EWK		
1B	EWK	"Palace"	
1C	EWK – MR		MR's pages are entitled "Piano Conductor."
1D	MR	"Sortie"	Page 4: last chord added in EWK's hand. After figure 15, EWK writes: "Segue Roder Sortie."
	EWK		2 pages of sketches.
1E	EWK		Pages seem out of order.
1F	EWK	"Robin Outside"	
2A	EWK	"Robin Entrance"	
2B	EWK	"Fight"	
2B	HWF		With alterations by EWK.
2C	HWF		With additions and deletions by EWK (originally went on longer).
3A	EWK	"The Killed"	
3B	EWK	"Meeting Robin-Little John"	
3C	EWK	"Fight with Little John"	
3D	EWK	"Gay Company"	
3E	EWK	"The Oath and The Black Arrow"	Then "see separate sheets."
3F	EWK	"The Fish"	
4A	EWK?	"Fight with Friar Tuck"	
4B	EWK	"A New Companion"	
4C	EWK		Shorthand refers back to "IIID."
5A	EWK	"Flirt"	
5B	EWK	"Das Treasure"	
5C	EWK	"Continuation"	Much of the cue is written in shorthand.
5D	EWK	"Gold"	
5E	EWK	"Triste"	
6A	EWK	"The Tournament"	
6B	EWK	"Robin Hood appears"	

Table 4.3. The Short Score (continued)

Cue	Hand	Title	Comments
	EWK		Page of sketches.
6C	EWK	"Preparation to [Fi]ght"	
6D	EWK	"Robin Hood Starts to Shoot"	
6E	EWK		Shorthand at figure 1 – "insert 15 bars of cue 6A."
7A			Missing.
7B	EWK	"The Trial"	
7C	EWK	"The Jail"	
7D	EWK	"The Gal-lows"	
8A	EWK	"The Fight"	
8B	EWK		
9A	EWK	"Arrest Marian"	
9B	MR	"Much"	End of first page: "Segue Reel A."
10A	MR		With additions by EWK.
10B	EWK		
10C	EWK	"Continua-tion"	At end: "Segue Roder."
			Page of sketches.
10D	EWK	"Nobile"	
10E	EWK		
11A	EWK	"Guy John"	
11B	EWK		
11C	EWK	"The Duell [*sic*, i.e., a mixture of English and German]"	
11D	EWK	"The Victory"	Shorthand references to 11C.
11E	EWK	"Epilogue"	At end: "Segue XIF Can't find."
11F			Missing.

shorthand markings refer the orchestrators to material to be inserted from an earlier cue: cues 1D, 3E, 4C and 9A, for example, all refer back to the earlier written cue 1C. There are a few instances, however, where the shorthand refers to cues later in the sequence: cue 1A, for example, refers to 1D; and 5C to 5D. Perhaps the most interesting examples of this phenomenon are the references to the love scene (8B) in cues 5E and 7C. Given that the sketches indicate the early completion of the love scene, this evidence seems to support the notion that 8B was one of the first cues to be worked out in its entirety (it was also one of the first to be recorded); Korngold could then plunder sections for other cues in the film. Table 4.3 summarizes the contents of the short score.

Full Score

There is some debate over the identity of those orchestrators who worked on the film since, aside from Friedhofer and Roder, Brendan Carroll mentions another figure, Reginald Bassett, in his Korngold biography:

> The release date was moved to 12 May 1938, but even so Korngold had only seven weeks to write [the score], supervise the orchestration (by Hugo Friedhofer, Milan Roder, and Reginald Basset [sic]), and then record the finished score.[24]

Again, in the liner notes for the Marco Polo CD, Carroll mentions Bassett, expanding the claim:

> The release date was moved to 12th May, but even so, Korngold had only seven weeks to write it, supervise the orchestration (by Hugo Friedhofer, Milan Roder and—for two short sequences—an assistant, Reginald Basset [sic]) and then record the finished score to the film.[25]

The claim has its origins in a letter that Friedhofer wrote to Rudy Behlmer. Carroll has speculated that Bassett was a lowly figure at Warner Bros. in 1938 and may have worked on the score without credit.[26] Certainly, I have found no written evidence in the manuscript sources to support this claim. Nor have I managed to identify a third hand in the full score, though there are passages where I cannot be entirely certain.[27] Admittedly, there are also pages missing from the full score that could conceivably have been penned by Bassett, but Friedhofer's letter to Behlmer must postdate the event by quite a number of years, and the possibility must be entertained that he remembered wrongly. In any event, Friedhofer talks at length about Bassett in his oral history (again, admittedly, many years later), mentioning the scores on which he worked with him (including *Intermezzo* and *Gone with the Wind*) and Bassett's association with Forbstein's predecessor at Warner Bros., Lou Silvers.[28] At no point does he mention Bassett's involvement with *The Adventures of Robin Hood*.

Whether the orchestrators worked directly from Korngold's short score or not is a question that also seems to create some confusion. As Friedhofer remembered:

> Jaro [Churain] had, from the time that Korngold first hit Hollywood, in connection with A MIDSUMMER NIGHT'S DREAM, been Korngold's amanuensis and copyist...I think he had probably known Jaro from Europe...Also, he [Churain] used to make the conductor parts from Korngold's sketches, because Korngold's handwriting, while it was perfectly legible, was very small...On Korngold films, with one exception, when we were in a terrible rush, and I had to work right from a sketch of Korngold's, I always worked from Churain's sketches.[29]

© 1974 American Film Institute.

Friedhofer confusingly seems to refer to Churain's "sketches" and "conductor parts" as if they were the same source; but, in any case, his statement is difficult to corroborate in the case of *The Adventures of Robin Hood*. The extant piano-conductor score for the film was certainly prepared after the full score had been written, since there are a number of orchestration markings in the piano-conductor version that are absent from the short score.[30] And, in the case of other piano-conductor scores, Robbert van der Lek has claimed that they were generally prepared by Charles Eggett and Anthony Macario.[31] The situation is further complicated by the pages of the short score that appear to have been copied by Hugo Friedhofer: at some stage, someone suspected that these pages are in Churain's hand. "Churain?" was written at the top of cue 2B and subsequently erased.

The full score, held at Warner Bros. archives, is largely complete. Each cue is bound individually into a book and stamped with a cue number and a reel identifier (with the number referring to the reel of film to which it belongs, and the letter to its position within the reel). A summary of its contents can be found in table 4.4.

Table 4.4. The Full Score

Cue number/ reel identifier	Master page numbers	Orchestrators[32]	Comments
1/1A			Missing.
2/1B			Missing.
3/1C	1–19	HWF/MR	
4/1D	20–32	HWF/MR	
5/1E	33–39	HWF	Pages 1–4 and 12 are missing.
6/1F	40–44	HWF	Strangely numbered 5–9 in pencil at bottom of pages.
7/2A	45–48	HWF	
8/2B	49–81	HWF/MR	
9/2C	82–108	HWF	
10/3A	109–111	HWF	
11/3B	112–126	HWF	
12/3C	127–134	HWF	
13/3D	135–142	HWF	
14/3E	143–158	HWF/MR	Has a separate title page.
15/3F	159–168	HWF	
16/4A	169–184	HWF	
17/4B	185–188	HWF	
18/4C	189–194	HWF	First six pages only (about 50 seconds of a 4.5-minute cue).
19/5A	195–205	HWF	
20/5B	206–223	HWF	
21/5C	224–232	HWF	
22/5D	233–241	HWF	
23/5E	242–260	HWF	
24/6A	261–273	MR	
25/6B	274–284	MR	
26/6C	285–288	MR	Only a Xerox copy.
27/6D	289–296	MR	
28/6E	297–325	MR	
29/7A	326–340	MR	Pages 329–334 are written on smaller manuscript paper of a green color.
30/7B	341–345	MR	
31/7C	346–354	MR/HWF	
32/7D	355–367	HWF	Page 355 is a Xerox.
33/8A	368–394	HWF	

Table 4.4 The Full Score (continued)

Cue number/ reel identifier	Master page numbers	Orchestrators	Comments
Liebes-Szene/8B	—	HWF	Not counted in master page sequence. The cue has no number.
35/9A	395–398	HWF	
36/9B	400[*sic*] – 404	MR	
37/10A	405–414	MR	
38/10B	415–425	HWF	
39/10C	426–440	HWF/MR	
40/10D	441–443	HWF	
/10E	444–447	HWF	Original version.
41/10E	448–466	HWF	
42/11A	467–478	MR	
43/11B	479–490	MR/HWF	
44/11C	491–504	HWF	Missing pages 1–4, 11–19, 25–28.
45/11D	505–509	MR	"The Victory" Missing after figure 7.
46/11E			Missing.
47/11F	510–513	HWF	Xerox.
48/Trailer I	514–515	MR	"Announcement" written on back of second page.
49/Trailer II	516–524	MR	
50/Trailer III	525–532	MR	
51/Trailer part 4	533–541	MR	

The manuscript paper used for each cue depends on who orchestrated it. Both Friedhofer and Roder used paper manufactured by the Kellaway-Ide Co. of Los Angeles, yet each opted for a different layout of preprinted instrument names. Friedhofer's layout[33] includes printed instrumentation as follows: flutes (2 staves); oboes (2 staves); clarinets (2 staves); bass clarinet; bassoons (2 staves); horns (2 staves); trumpets (2 staves); trombones (2 staves); tuba; "timpani etc." (2 staves); vibraphone; harp; piano and celeste [*sic*]; blank stave; violin (2 staves); viola (2 staves); cello (2 staves); bass. Roder's printed instrumentation differs slightly: flutes (2 staves); oboes (2 staves); clarinets (2 staves); bassoons (2 staves); horns (2 staves); trumpets (2 staves); trombones and tuba (2 staves); "timpani, etc." (1 stave); "drums, etc." (1 line);

harp; piano or celeste [*sic*]; violin (2 staves); viola (2 staves); cello (2 staves); bass. In addition, Roder's pages are much narrower than Friedhofer's and are colored a banana yellow.

The consistent use of their own paper suggests a certain independence from each other, and there is no evidence that the two orchestrators collaborated at all. Indeed at one point in cue 2B, both orchestrated the same passage. Roder's main contribution was the central archery tournament, but there are cues where both Friedhofer and Roder have contributed pages; it was essential, therefore, that their styles were compatible. While Friedhofer in his oral history gives tantalizing glimpses of his working relationship with Korngold, there are no corresponding passages to suggest he enjoyed any extended contact with Roder at all:

> ATKINS: What was Roder's function? Was he on the lot?
> FRIEDHOFER: No, he wasn't on the lot permanently, but he used to be called in. He was a sort of free lance orchestrator around town.[34]

© 1974 American Film Institute.

Apart from the cues heard in the film, the full score also includes material used for the film's trailer. Its four sections were prepared by Milan Roder and recorded contemporaneously with the rest of the score. The first section, cue number 48, does not appear in the trailer as it exists today—though it does appear in the trailer for *Dodge City*—and, apart from the latter half of cue number 50, much of the music is inaudible in the sound mix. The source of the trailer music is summarized in table 4.5.

Frustratingly, the full score continued to be used after the recording of the cues. While its use for preparing a narrated radio broadcast of the music (of which more below) and a Symphonic Suite for use in concert performances by Korngold is of considerable interest, Charles Gerhardt also used it in 1974 when preparing his own recording of extracts from the score. Numerous markings exist in both the full score and parts that refer to the "1974 session" and which correspond with the recording found on the RCA LP entitled *Captain Blood: Classic Film Scores for Errol Flynn*.[35]

Numerous other cuts are also marked in this full score that correspond with the final edit of the film. As conducting markings are also much in evidence, it seems safe to conclude that, unlike the usual practice at Warner Bros., Korngold used the full score to conduct during the sessions with the orchestra. Several cues include revised sections that appear to have been changed after the film's Pomona sneak preview, and numerous other minor changes also appear to have been made: some of these occurred during the orchestration process; others during the scoring sessions themselves.

Table 4.5. Trailer Music

Section	Source
48/Trailer I	G-major fanfare from cue 1E reorchestrated with less percussion.
49/Trailer II	Opens with an original fanfare by Roder and 2 bars of re-orchestrated material from 10D; instruction to copy from 10D bars 2–9; transposed material from figures 26–31 in 8B.
50/Trailer III	8B from figure 21 to figure 24; 8B from bar 2 of figure 5 to bar before figure 7; 4 original chords.
51/Trailer "part 4" [*sic*]	Copied from 1D, figure 7 to figure 9; reorchestrated from 1D, figure 10 to the bar before figure 14; "new bar"; first 3 bars from cue 2B; 33 bars copied from 8A, figures 2 to 8 (using "old parts"); re-orchestrated section of *Sursum Corda* from 8 before figure 3 to figure 3; copied from 2B figure 1 for 5 bars; copied from 11B for 2 bars (5 before end of cue); last 3 bars presumably taken from missing cue 11D.

Piano-Conductor Score and Orchestral Parts

Upon completion of the full score for a cue, copyists working at Warner Bros.—including Albert Glasser, Art Grier, and someone referred to in the full score as "Vito"—prepared the orchestral parts and the piano-conductor score. The latter was prepared as standard procedure, even though Korngold would conduct from the full score, and was used to document many of the changes made during the scoring sessions and to prepare the music clearance sheet, or 'cue sheet' (not to be confused with Korngold's own cue sheets), which details copyright permissions.

The original piano-conductor score is kept at Warner Bros. studios in Burbank and is an almost complete copy of the score reduced to short score format; other blue 'ditto' copies are found with the orchestral parts at Warner Bros. archives. The manuscript was prepared by a number of different hands, based on the format of Korngold's short score but incorporating changes made during orchestration, and contains a number of variants from both the full and short scores.

Throughout the manuscript are a series of letters and numbers, running from YM 5325-9032-1 to YM 5922-12-2+4 that refer to the recording take used to assemble the final music track. They give the order in which the score was recorded and are summarized in the table in the appendix. It seems likely that this piano-conductor score was used by the person in charge of the recording process, probably Leo Forbstein, rather than Korngold himself. Korngold did see a copy of the score and made some minor changes to dynamics before passing it back to Forbstein for use in the sessions. The manuscript also contains a number of descriptive labels for the various musical themes, such as "Robin Hood Hero" or "Richard the Lion Heart." Though the themes are not always referred to consistently, these labels are reproduced in the cue sheet that is stored along with the manuscript at Burbank Studios. Dated 29 April 1938, this cue sheet contains details of the music's composer and publisher, its timings, and how it is used in each reel (whether "partial" or "entire," used as "backing" or "visual instrumental"). It seems to be a generic form that could be used for any source music, allowing it to be cleared for copyright purposes. Finally, stored with the piano-conductor score are a number of written sheets with information that appears to have been used to prepare both the 1938 and the 1948 re-release trailers.

In terms of the orchestral parts, each cue for each part is bound separately using tape so that the pages could be folded out, necessitating as few turns as possible for the musicians. Particularly useful in tracing the recording of the score are the dates that Teddy Krise wrote on his part when he was involved, dates that are reproduced in the appendix. Krise, it appears, was a clarinetist (generally playing 2nd or 3rd clarinet) who also played alto saxophone and, on one occasion (in cue 3E), oboe and cor anglais. Also of interest are the numerous doodles and word games with which the bored session musicians of the Warner Bros. orchestra entertained themselves. In a double bass part for cue 10E, for example, a player had evidently tried to keep spirits up with a practical joke, which he noted down for posterity: "Note: put mute in mouth, appear to choke."

Radio Show

The radio show, which can be heard on the DVD, was broadcast by radio station KECA and the NBC Blue Network at 7:30 p.m. on 11 May 1938.[36] It presented certain extracted parts of the score, played by the Warner Bros. orchestra conducted by Korngold, with accompanying narration by actor Basil Rathbone. Warner Bros. initially intended to release it commercially, but these plans were abandoned.[37]

Table 4.6. Summary of Radio Show Sources

Extract	Musical source
Opening fanfare	1E fanfare at figure 6
The Theme of the Merry Men	1A (main title)
Banquet at Nottingham	1E (shortened) / Symphonic Suite 1st movement without fanfares and figures 5 to 6
Robin's Entrance	1F; 2C figures 7 to 23, figure 27 to the end
Little John's Meeting	3B opening to figure 3, figures 9 to 11; 3C with altered opening
Friar Tuck	3F figure 1 to (slightly altered) end
Attack on Sir Guy	Part of 4C / Symphonic Suite 2nd movement beginning at figure 8
Feast and the Flirtation	5B, opening until figure 8; 5C with extra bar added at end
The Gallows and Escape	7D opening to figure 5; Trailer 4 figure 6, bar 2 until end (itself adapted from 8A, 2B, 11B and 11E)
Lady Marian's Heartsong	8B figure 7 until end (cutting the 3rd and 4th bars of figure 10)
"It is victory!"	11C / Symphonic Suite 4th movement opening to figure 22 (with cut at figure 4); 11D figure 7 to end (cutting figures 12 to 13)
"and so, the legend of Robin Hood lives on forever"	11E / Symphonic Suite 4th movement figure 26 to the end

Eight pressings were made by KFWB on four records for Korngold and a number of studio executives. Writing in 1997, Brendan Carroll claimed that of the eight sets made, only three were known to have survived: one was in the Korngold estate; one was in the possession of copyist Albert Glasser; and the third was in Carroll's own collection, a gift from Teddy Krise who had purchased a set of the discs from Tenny Wright, Warner's studio production manager.[38] I learned in 2003, however, that John Newton of the Vitaphone Project also has an incomplete set. Although Carroll claims that the music constitutes "virtually the entire score,"[39] there is much that is missing, and of the cues that are present, nearly all have been subjected to alteration. There is also evidence to indicate that the full score manuscript was prepared carefully for Korngold in advance of the broadcast, and Carroll notes that copyist Glasser was on hand, presumably at the rehearsal, to iron out any problems with the parts. Of interest, too, is the close resemblance between versions of some of the cues and the Symphonic Suite. As the Symphonic Suite's first performance postdates the radio show, it seems likely that either Korngold used the radio show as the basis of his suite or the two versions were prepared almost simultaneously. Table 4.6 summarizes the contents of the radio show.

Symphonic Suite

Shortly after the film premièred on 12 May, Korngold arranged a Symphonic Suite consisting of four movements: *Alt England* (Old England); *Robin Hood und Seine Fröhliche Schar* (Robin Hood and His Merry Men); *Liebes-Szene* (Love Scene); and *Kampf, Sieg und Epilog* (The Fight, Victory and Epilogue). It was prepared for a concert on 24 June 1938 in Oakland, California, that Korngold conducted with the Bay Region Symphony Orchestra.[40] A Xerox copy of the Suite was deposited in the Warner Bros. archives by George Korngold, the composer's son, to replace those parts of the score that were missing. In fact, many of the missing sections of the full score correspond exactly with the material used in the Suite, suggesting that the full score manuscript was plundered specifically in order to prepare this concert version of the music.

John Morgan has claimed that the Symphonic Suite was reorchestrated, eliminating extra woodwind and brass, reducing the percussion from five to three players, combining piano and celesta parts, and integrating two harp parts into one.[41] Without the missing sections of the score, though, this statement is difficult to corroborate. Of the sections that can be compared, no differences in the orchestration can be found, aside from some alternative instrumentations in the *Liebes-Szene*: at figure 7, for example, the alto saxophone line has been doubled in cor anglais with a note in Korngold's hand that reads "if no Sxph [Saxophone]"; similarly at figure 13, "EH [English Horn] if [no] Sxph," and later at figure 26, "Cl1 [1st Clarinet] if no Sxph." Finally, at the fourth of figure 27, the trumpet takes the saxophone part.

Adaptation of Preexisting Material

Sursum Corda

While working on *Die tote Stadt* in the summer of 1919, Korngold composed a symphonic overture for large orchestra that he dedicated to Richard Strauss. Entitled *Sursum Corda* (which translates as "lift up your hearts"),[42] it was to have a sizable impact on the score for *The Adventures of Robin Hood* and would feature in it prominently. The overture was a rare flop for Korngold when first performed by the Vienna Symphony Orchestra under the composer's baton on 24 January 1920.[43] A few years later while in Rome, Korngold signed the guest book at a restaurant with themes from *Sursum Corda* and his incidental music for *Much Ado about Nothing*. Next to the first he wrote "Hissed"; next to the second "Applauded"; and underneath, "In a hundred years, may be the other way around."[44] The overture was published by B. Schott's Söhne, Mainz, in 1921 under the title *Sinfonische Ouvertüre ("Sursum Corda!") für grosses Orchester* as Korngold's Op. 13.

Example 4.6. Robin's Theme

Korngold's faith in *Sursum Corda*, which has never achieved lasting success as a concert piece, was such that when Julius suggested using it as the theme for the "captain of the brigands" in *Robin Hood*, Korngold wrote to his publishers and requested he be granted permission to use the overture in the score. Its main motif doubles as the theme for Robin himself (example 4.6) and appears in an altered version as the "Jollity" theme (examples 4.7 and 4.8), while another variant of the main motif becomes the love theme (examples 4.9 and 4.10). A precursor to the rising ninths of Sir Guy's theme (see example 4.11) is also found at figure 13. *Sursum Corda* thus pervades virtually the entire score.

Example 4.7. "Jollity"

Example 4.8. Intervallic Links between Robin's Theme and "Jollity"

In addition, large sections of the overture were extracted and reused for the battle scenes in cues 2B, 7A, 8A, and 11B. A summary of this material can be seen in table 4.7. Hugo Friedhofer was charged with adapting these sections, and he did so with the published score in his hand. Where possible, he seems to have copied directly from the score, even copying in a slur that makes no sense in the context of the cue.[45]

Example 4.9. The Love Theme

Example 4.10. Intervallic Links between Robin's Theme and the Love Theme

Example 4.11 Sir Guy's Theme

Friedhofer's role was much more than just a copyist, though; the orchestration of 8A, for example, required a good deal of rescoring to fit the available forces of the Warner Bros. orchestra. *Sursum Corda* is scored for a large orchestra with three violin parts and instruments such as the bass trumpet, and to fit the smaller string section and compensate for missing instruments, Friedhofer was forced to reorchestrate practically every bar, albeit only subtly. Cue 2B is a particularly interesting example of this. The section when Robin makes for the door and the call rings out "Open the door!" was originally orchestrated by Friedhofer based on the passage found in *Sursum Corda*. After the parts were copied, however, it was clearly felt to be inadequate in the context of the scene, and Milan Roder stepped in with a much more heavily scored version. Some heavy cuts were also made at this stage, with the full score showing the evidence of these; this took the final version of 2B used, recorded on or around 4 March, further from the *Sursum Corda* original.

Table 4.7. Use of *Sursum Corda* in *Robin Hood*

Cue/Theme	Source in published version of *Sursum Corda*
Robin's theme	Bs 2-6
Love theme	Figure 17 to 8 after 18
2B	Figures 3 to 5; 3rd bar of figure 25 to figure 33
7A	Figure 3 to figure 5
8A	Beginning to 8 before figure 3; figure 21 to 6 before 24
11B	"Festes Zeitmaß" after figure 46 to figure 49

It also seems likely that Friedhofer, at Korngold's instruction, re-orchestrated these sections of the overture before a decision had been made as to where they would be placed. Cue 11B, for example, consists mainly of *Sursum Corda* material, with a new beginning, a new ending, and added first/second time bars to allow for a repeat. While the *Sursum Corda* pages are in Friedhofer's hand, the new sections are orchestrated by Roder. In addition, Roder writes at the top of Friedhofer's first page, "XI-B page 2," which suggests that Friedhofer's orchestration of this passage was extant when Roder prepared the rest of the cue from Korngold's short score.

Cue 8A demonstrates some of the complexities of this adaptation process, as well as the difficulties for the musicologist in trying to trace this procedure. Korngold's short score combines passages of new notated music with written indications that point Friedhofer to the relevant section from *Sursum Corda* from which to extract the rest of the cue. Thus after the first five bars, Korngold indicates that 33 bars should be taken from the beginning until page 6 of the published Schott edition of *Sursum Corda*. Aside from the first bar, therefore, no music from the opening of the overture is written out. There then follows a "New" section of music, which is sketched in full, before a piece of text again indicates that the next section should be taken from the existing work (this time, 17 bars, though with no obvious indication of the start point). Following four bars of "New" material at figure 14, Korngold writes "Sursum pag[e] 34" but this time underneath a written out melody line (see example 4.12).

Looking at the full score, we do indeed find that after the first five bars, there are 33 bars that have been taken from the beginning of *Sursum Corda* as per Korngold's first written instruction; however, from the beginning of *Sursum Corda* until the point on page 6 where the orchestrators stop was originally a passage of some 36 bars, not 33. Three bars of *Sursum Corda*, namely, bars 23, 26, and 33, are absent from cue 8A. What happened to these? All three 'missing' bars function similarly in the overture: they extend the melody by an extra bar and, being harmonically static, can therefore be easily removed without threatening the musical coherence of the passage. The second of these bars *was* orchestrated but subsequently cut out of the full score (there is a gap in the manuscript). This perhaps indicates a mistake on Friedhofer's part or is evidence of a new picture edit requiring the excision of a bar. As this bar doesn't feature in any of the session masters nor in the piano conductor score, it seems safe to conclude that it was removed at some point before the recording process. The question remains for the analyst, though: how did Friedhofer know which bars of the 36 to cut to bring it down to the total of 33? Was this information provided verbally by Korngold or recorded in writing somewhere else?

One possible answer seems to be provided by Korngold's written-out *Sursum Corda* section in the short score at figure 15. This section derives from a passage on page 34 of *Sursum Corda* that includes a reiterated melody with a bar of the same rhythm as the ones cut by Friedhofer. Crucially, though, when Korngold writes out the melody in the piano short score, he leaves out the equivalent bar on both occasions, in effect setting a precedent for Friedhofer to follow in the earlier sections (see example 4.12).

The other 17-bar section of *Sursum Corda* (found between figures 11 and 14 in the full score) also proves somewhat mysterious. The relevant section in *Sursum Corda* (found on pages 32–33 in the Schott edition) is actually 16 bars long. Friedhofer's version in the full score augments the last bar, stretching it to fill two bars instead of one. Whether this was agreed verbally between Korngold and Friedhofer as an alternative to the "*poco rit*" indication in *Sursum Corda* or represents some sort of miscounting can only be speculated.

Example 4.12. *Sursum Corda* **in Cue 8A**

Rosen aus Florida

In 1928, still reeling slightly from the *Heliane-Jonny spielt auf* affair, Korngold returned to Viennese operetta and set about completing Leo Fall's operetta *Rosen aus Florida*, which had been left unfinished at the composer's death in 1925, for a production at the Theater an der Wien on 22 February 1929. According to Brendan Carroll, Korngold composed most of the second act himself in the style of Fall.[46] As part of the Act 2 finale, he wrote a seventeen-bar waltz entitled "Miß Austria" as part of a "Schönheitskonkurrenz der Nationen" or "beauty contest of nations" (see example 4.13).[47] This short, lighthearted parody of his homeland's musical style, like *Sursum Corda* before it, was to prove particularly useful when writing the music for *The Adventures of Robin Hood* a decade later. "Miß Austria" is heard in virtually its original form, albeit in a different key and tempo, in the banquet scenes in Sherwood (see example 4.14).

It is also adapted as the March of the Merry Men, a theme that appears throughout the score and opens and closes the film (example 4.15). Thus in either its waltz or march form, "Miß Austria" can be heard in the following cues: 1A; 3D; 4B; 4C; 5B (in waltz form); 5C (waltz); 5D (waltz); 6B; 6D; 10E; 11D; and 11F.

Example 4.13. "Miß Austria"

Example 4.14. The Banquet Waltz

Example 4.15. The March of the Merry Men

Die Kathrin

When Korngold started work on *The Adventures of Robin Hood* in the summer of 1937, he was partway through completing the orchestration of his fifth opera, *Die Kathrin*, and anxiously trying to arrange its pre-mière in Vienna. Originally planned for the 1937–1938 season at the Staatsoper (the Hofoper post 1918) to be conducted by Korngold's great friend, Bruno Walter, *Die Kathrin* suffered a number of setbacks: Jan Kiepura, for example, had to withdraw from the main role of Fran-çois due to commitments with the Metropolitan Opera in New York. When Korngold left Vienna in January 1938, though, he did so with the promise of a Viennese première in October with Richard Tauber and Jarmila Novotná. Political tensions intervened, however, but thanks to the publishers Weinberger—who not only took over publication from the politically hand-tied Schott but also rescued the score before Korn-gold's property was confiscated by the Nazis—a production was ar-ranged in Sweden. The première thus took place on 7 October 1939, but it was received poorly by the press, some of whom branded the opera "Jewish filth."[48]

It is perhaps unsurprising, given its contemporaneous origin, that much of the musical language and style of *Kathrin* should bear a pass-ing resemblance to *Robin Hood*. Carroll has always pointed out the similarity of Prince John's fanfare to the fanfares heard at figures 13 and 18 in its first scene.[49] Other features of the first act of the opera, though, can also be traced in the film score. With its military setting, *Kathrin* uses a number of marches that have superficial resonances with the March of the Merry Men, especially as Korngold turns the student's march of scene iv into a waltz at figure 187, much as he was to do with the film's march. Similarly, the fanfares heard in scene iv of Act 1 are reminiscent of Robin's fanfare theme. Undoubtedly these affinities are the result of similar militaristic subject matters; indeed, the march heard in the *Zwischenspiel* of scene iv also bears a resemblance to the chorus of street boys and the Act 2 entr'acte from *Carmen*, in addition to the coronation procession from *Robin Hood*. Even the love theme from *Robin Hood* seems to be paralleled in the shape of certain phrases in Francois's "Es ist ja wahr" from Act 1 and the dialogue that follows between Kathrin and Margot.

Identifying the Film Score

The evidence presented above suggests that the task of identifying the 'film score' is indeed a difficult one. The radio show, for instance, purports to present Korngold's score, yet it restores some bars left out in the final cut of the movie, while simultaneously cutting large sections. Could we simply ignore these other versions, though, and label the music heard in the film itself as the 'film score'? We might wonder if there has been just one version, though; can we talk about 'the film' as a singular source? Fortunately, the evidence seems to suggest that once the picture was released on 12 May 1938 it remained in the same cut of 102 minutes in its subsequent release for commercial video, DVD, and television (for the PAL color system, this equates to 98 minutes, as the film runs at 25 rather than 24 frames per second). This is in stark contrast to many pictures of this era that were trimmed for TV presentation.[50] Nor is there any suggestion of any further editing when *The Adventures of Robin Hood* was re-released in 1948 with a new Technicolor print, or when it was reissued in black-and-white in the mid-1950s before being sold to television.[51]

Although the edit of *Robin Hood* remains consistent (we assume), there are a number of ways in which this released edit of the film differs from the version of the cues recorded in the studio and notated in the manuscript sources. There were a number of cuts made to the music track after the recording sessions had taken place, cuts that are not indicated in the full score. These must have occurred at a relatively late stage in postproduction and are perhaps indicative of some last-minute tinkering in the image by Hal Wallis, possibly in response to the Pomona sneak preview. In cue 2B, for example, one of these edits had a rather detrimental effect on the internal logic of the music (see example 2.1).

Yet, beyond these slight alterations, there were also a large number of revisions that were made to the score at various stages,[52] including some changes made after the Pomona sneak preview. An alternate version of the film, with a different score, did therefore exist at a particular historical moment for a particular audience. These post-Pomona changes, which warranted another recording session on 11 April, included revisions to cues 8A, 9A, 10A, 10B, 10C, and 10E. While the revisions to 9A (sustaining the last chord much longer) and 10A and 10B (thicker orchestration) were relatively minor, the changes made to the other cues result in quite different viewing/listening experiences. The original version of 10C can be heard in track 19 of the Tsunami

CD (available only in Europe as TSU0139), while the original ending of 8A can be experienced through the DVD's music-only audio track.

Cue 8A, in fact, had three endings at various points in its history (see examples 4.16–4.18).[53] The original ending exists in Korngold's short score, the full score, and the piano-conductor score. At some point, however, an alternative ending, designed to replace its last three bars, was composed. This alternative exists in the full score and the piano-conductor score and was recorded on 11 April (as 8A retake "made wild"). The version heard in the film itself, however, is a third ending that replaced only the last bar of the original. No recording information exists for this version, and it is perhaps conceivable that it was adapted from the 11 April retake by artificially lengthening the chord at the beginning of that version's penultimate bar.[54] Interestingly, neither of these later changes to the end, nor any of the 11 April revisions, are extant in any of the manuscript sources in Korngold's hand.

Which ending, then, constitutes part of the film score? Can we really claim that any one of them has more of a right to be considered the 'correct' version? By claiming that the original ending is the only one to be ascribed categorically to Korngold, we betray a certain ideological attachment to the composer's intentions and ignore the fact that the third ending is the one with which the vast majority of audiences are familiar. Similarly, by accepting this third ending as the proper ending of cue 8A, we ignore the interest of both the original and the second endings. The only sensible answer, it would seem, is to regard all the versions of the music as equally suitable for inclusion under the umbrella term of 'the film score.' The film score thus reveals its inherently Text-like pluralism.

Composing a film score, then, cannot be characterized as a straightforward act of composition in the way that most music in the Western classical tradition, until relatively recently, has been presented: it appears to be a fluid, multistage process that involves numerous creative personas and depends, for a large part, on changes made to the film's visuals. While there are undoubtedly precedents for this kind of composition in opera and ballet, the realities of studio-era film score production are a far cry from the romanticized view of authorship that many commentators, and even film composers themselves,[55] have tried to invoke. In the specific case of *The Adventures of Robin Hood*, much of the material 'composed' existed in some form before the film was even conceived, though it had never been used in another film score; the music thus already carried a wealth of accrued cultural associations with Viennese operetta, the concert music of a child prodigy, and the rhythms and phraseology of Elizabethan balladry, before it was ever tied to a Warner Bros. swashbuckler. Though all music carries a degree of this cultural baggage around openly, the score to *The Adventures of Robin Hood* has a remarkably wide cultural footprint for one that is frequently held up by defenders of a romantic aesthetic of composition as one of the great movie scores (presumably in contrast to the hack work of 'assembly-line' composers at Universal, for example). Its qualities are not in doubt, yet in tying them to the received picture of Korngold (as the great and, until recently, undervalued composer), these romantics do a disservice both to the wide-ranging circumstances of the score's origins and to those creative figures who lent a hand to bring the score to the viewing public.

Example 4.16. Original Ending for Cue 8A

Example 4.17. Alternative Ending for Cue 8A (11 April Retake)

Example 4.18. Ending for Cue 8A Used in the Film

5

ANALYSIS AND
READINGS OF THE SCORE

If the preceding chapters have fragmented the unitary voice of Korngold and suggested the presence of other authorial voices, this chapter
aims to reconstruct what Edward T. Cone called the "complete musical
persona."[1] Rather than a single author, though—allied with the notion
of a composer's intentions—this complete musical persona can be seen
as a construction of authorial voices achieved through the presence of
the music's interpreter, namely, a member of the film's audience. As
Roland Barthes revealed in his groundbreaking analysis of narrative
S/Z, reading is far from a passive activity; rather, it is a kind of writing
that, through the weaving of different critical voices, creates the Text.[2]
The reader's role, then, is potentially hugely significant in creating
meaning. Yet, is this really how film music works? Is each individual's
response to a film score unique, or are there certain universal responses
that film composers depend upon, codified as film score conventions?
It seems the answer may lie somewhere between the two states, so that
the individual subject and universal response exist ostensibly in a state
of dialectical tension.

Certainly the 'rhythm' of an individual's reading cannot be pre-
dicted; for Barthes, the 'Pleasure of the Text' lies partly in what is
"read and not read" in a classical narrative.[3] This 'tmesis' is never the
same on each reading; what the reader chooses to gloss over, the
rhythm of his/her reading, is unpredictable. The film score, thanks to
the advances in home entertainment, can now be the subject of repeated
rereadings with no degradation in viewing quality.[4] But what the listener chooses to focus his/her attention on in the sound mix is just as
unpredictable. Can music really be 'read,' though, in the sense that we

'understand' the meanings of a piece of written text? Traditionally, music has been regarded as a nonrepresentational art, a far less stable semiotic system than language; yet, as the poststructuralist approach of Barthes, Derrida, and Foucault recognized, language itself is far from stable in the relationship between signifier and signified. Similarly, the resistance to using language to describe or explain music demonstrated by the neo-positivist musicologists of the mid-twentieth century, intent on emphasizing music's ineffable qualities, has ebbed away. Lawrence Kramer can thus acknowledge that "language cannot capture musical experience," but he also argues that this is precisely because "it cannot capture any experience whatever, including the experience of language itself"[5] and talks about music ekphrastically (using language to describe it rather than relying on 'cold' analytical techniques).[6] Such attitudes are reflected in the boom in musical hermeneutics, evinced in the New or Critical Musicology, that proceeds from the assumption that music means something beyond the beauty of its structure; that it can be historically, culturally, and socially situated; and that these worldly qualities can be detected in the music. While the interaction of music with more representational information contained in the dialogue and visuals of film allows us to sidestep some of these issues, which are potentially more problematic for so-called autonomous music genres like the symphony or string quartet, it does provide us with a safe territory in which to address the question of musical meaning.

The primary role of musical hermeneutics, in Kramer's formulation at least, is "to make music a medium of alliance: to promote collaboration, establish a socially resonant interplay of consensus and contention, and form or enrich intimacy or group identity."[7] And yet the overarching impression of Kramer's book *Musical Meaning: Toward a Critical History* is of a personal baring of the soul that includes not only references to a painful familial history[8] but also the author's own composition, which he includes as a compact disc appendix.[9] This tension between the individual response and a sense of group identity is arguably a major factor in the way film music works. It is, after all, a highly codified language that, although unable to predict a response in the spectator, works precisely because we respond to it in similar ways. This chapter will therefore examine the tension between the notion of convention, examining those elements of the score to *The Adventures of Robin Hood* that have been seen to typify the 'classic Hollywood film score' and established a model for others to follow, and a more individual response created through a Barthesian kind of rereading, rich with intertextual references. The weave of textual voices that is created by

the reader encompasses this tension and will allow for the detailed examination of a scene from the film. Finally, an assessment of Korngold's place within this tension, and some broader conclusions about
the way we might read film scores, will be proposed.

Convention and
The Adventures of Robin Hood

Thematicism and Character Identity

As is common in other scores of the period, and in other Korngold
films, the music of *The Adventures of Robin Hood* is structured the-
matically. Themes are associated both with characters and, less dis-
tinctly, with concepts; in the case of three of these themes (Robin,
Richard, and the love theme), they also undergo a certain amount of
development, eventually culminating in a fusing together that parallels
the narrative climax of the film.

There are eight principal themes (the March of the Merry Men,
Robin, Jollity, King Richard/England, Love, Marian, Sir Guy, Oppression) with a further five (Prince John, Horses, Flirt, English Air, Friar
Tuck) playing a more minor role. The intended recognition of these
thematic associations plays a major part in clarifying the course of the
film's narrative and in establishing character identity. They can thus be
considered part of a universal response, which relies comparatively less
on intertextual links with other Texts than other more individual-driven
readings. While an assessment of the 'appropriateness' of the themes to
the characters or concepts with which they are associated is arguably
far more dependent on other Texts, the associations themselves do not
seem to require any knowledge beyond the perceived boundaries of the
score. As has been suggested in chapter 4, though, these boundaries can
be considered something of an illusion, and the implications of an intertextual reading for the following thematic analysis are always threatening to break through.

Similarly, the question of whose voice is speaking through these
themes is a difficult one to conceptualize. A conventional approach
might argue that this is the voice of the composer, responding to the
characters as he sees them. Korngold thus becomes a narrating voice,
able to comment on the characters' foibles and stand between the film's
audience and the filmmakers. Such an attitude, however, although shar-

ing much in common with the chronology of the score's production, has the potential to close off meaning. Instead, we might potentially interpret the themes as evidence of the characters' own musical voices that Korngold merely allows to speak through him. While these voices are 'imagined' by Korngold during the production process, once wedded to the rest of the film they arguably become as 'real' as any other musical voice experienced. In any case, it is clear that this thematic approach to scoring a film was one of the factors that distinguished the Korngold/Steiner model of the classical era of film and what composers like John Williams looked to revive in the 1970s.

March of the Merry Men

The first theme to be introduced is the March of the Merry Men (see example 4.15). This theme is broadly associated with Robin's band of men and reappears throughout the film in various guises. In its simplest form, heard in the main (1A, see table 4.1) and end titles (11F) in B-flat major and F major, respectively, it acts as a frame for the rest of the score, maintaining a children's storybook quality through its optimistic tone, heroic brass-and-strings orchestration, and uncomplicated diatonicism. Some of the set pieces of the Robin Hood legend also feature the March, further adding to this fictive quality. In cue 3D, for example, as Robin and Little John climb back onto the bank after their quarterstaff fight, we hear the March scored for violas and bassoons: here, the ranks of Robin's Merry Men are still confined to Will Scarlett and the newly inducted Little John, and the March therefore warrants a smaller orchestration that relies on tenor instruments to match Little John's stature. Similarly, when Friar Tuck joins the band in 4B, a *Moderato* version of the March is scored for solo bassoon (in best comic fashion to parody Tuck's ample frame), pizzicato strings, and percussion, in Korngold's favorite key of F-sharp major (virtually its only appearance in the entire score). As the other Merry Men hail the newest member of their band, first clarinets then strings enter, allowing the March to stand for the multiple voices of Robin's followers. The attack on the treasure caravan (cue 4C) also begins with the same March theme, this time scored much in the manner of the opening and closing titles, as Robin's men make preparations for the ambush.

The March of the Merry Men is, however, subjected to a certain amount of variation. As Robin and his band appear in disguise at the archery tournament in cue 6B, we hear the theme's melody also partially disguised (see example 5.1). The disguise is maintained for only the first two phrases of the March, until Robin berates his men for their cautious approach. The risk and adventure that he craves are achieved musically by throwing off the disguise and revealing the March of the Merry Men for all to hear. Similarly in cue 10E, the procession to Nottingham Castle for the film's climactic coronation ceremony, we hear the theme in B-flat minor. As such, it clearly identifies the monks on screen as the disguised members of Robin's band, though, as in earlier cues, their disguise warrants a degree of musical camouflage. In this way, it prompts a universal response in the spectator: we are expected to recognize the significance of this theme and therefore the characters that it signals. By the end of the cue, with the procession safely inside the castle, the March settles into an optimistic B-flat major, with Little John (and the music) giving Much (and the audience) a reassuring wink. As the Bishop of the Black Canons, coerced by Robin, questions Prince John's authority in the next cue, another variant of the March theme is heard as if to remind us of the power behind his question.

The most obvious variant of this theme, though, is its transformation into a waltz during the banquet scenes in Sherwood (in cues 5C and 5D; see example 4.14). At this point within the musical logic of the thematic and narrative structure, its 'disguise' could be read as reflecting the change in Robin's band as they relax in the safety of their camp. As will be discussed below, an awareness of the score's intertextuality at this point will suggest other readings.

King Richard/England - Robin - Jollity - Love

These four themes are closely linked, and their interactions and development constitutes the structural heart of the score. The themes themselves—and their growing associations—will be outlined first, before their combinations and developments are discussed.

The theme associated with King Richard, and by extension England, is first heard in the main titles (1A) as the first narrative intertitle is displayed (see example 5.2). Though its associations are not immediately clear, the unambiguous nature of the E-flat-major harmony immediately evokes a safe, unchallenging, old-world romanticism with none of the harmonic angst that will characterize Sir Guy's theme or the knife fight between Much and Dickon later in the film. Indeed it initially seems to stand simply for the 'once upon a time' nostalgia of the story; only as the film progresses does it accrue its meanings.

Example 5.1. Merry Men Disguise

The theme is heard throughout large sections of the film, but is mostly fragmented or varied somehow with different orchestration or in a different key. It is as if the characters borrow the voice of the absent Richard to invoke all that he stands for. It is next heard in cue 3E when Robin asks his new followers to swear an oath to uphold his values. It appears in an ambivalent G major/minor and only settles into G major after six bars, when talk turns to fighting for a free England and the return of Richard. The theme thus gradually becomes associated with Robin's cause and his loyalty to Richard. During the feast scene in Sherwood (5D), Marian questions Robin's intentions. In response to her criticisms, he asks his men what they should do with the treasure they have captured: "Divide it among ourselves?" The men respond: "Hold it for Richard. It belongs to the King!" His question is set to the first phrase of Richard's theme in E-flat major; the answer shifts the B-flat up a semitone. Then the phrase resolves into a D major full statement of Richard's theme as the men show their loyalty, and Marian begins to soften in her attitude (see example 5.3).

Example 5.2. Richard's Theme

Example 5.3. Richard's Theme in 5D

As Robin and Marian visit the poor people and she struggles to under-stand his ethics in cue 5E, Richard's theme appears again. When she points out that "one of those men was a Norman," Robin's reply—"Norman or Saxon. What's that matter? It's injustice I hate, not the Normans"—is accompanied by Richard's theme in B major on a solo cello, implicitly connecting Richard—and, by extension, Robin—with the restoration of social justice. Indeed, the solo line seems to link this universal ideal of England and its values with an individual: it is Robin who is propounding his value system, and it therefore seems logical to suggest that Robin has adopted Richard's voice, and his theme, at this point. Richard's theme is then absent for the darkest parts of the film in which Robin is captured and sentenced to death. His rescue and the declaration of love between Robin and Marian prompts its reappear-ance (8B). Again it is heard on a solo cello. The last bars of the cue are heard over the dissolve to the sign for Kent Road Tavern and feature the opening of the theme, thus giving the audience a clue as to the iden-tity of the disguised travelers inside.

It is in reel 10, though, that Richard's theme is most present, and where it now starts to delineate the physical presence of Richard him-self (in 10B, 10C, and 10D). As Richard, still disguised, converses with Robin, the last phrase is developed sequentially for the first time (see example 5.4), before we hear another extension to the theme, heard previously in 5D and the love scene (8B); again it seems the disguise prevents Richard's voice from speaking clearly. We hear the theme in its most familiar guise as Robin berates Richard (who he still assumes to be in the Holy Lands) for deserting his people; still, though, it is as-sociated as much with the idea of Richard as the character himself, and its modulation to F major and sudden interruption by a move to the flattened submediant prevent its resolution. Only when he removes his disguise does Richard appear finally to take ownership of his own mu-sic: the theme is heard in a *nobile* E-flat major rendition, and at a slower tempo than any other point (cue 10D). Here we are presented with the rightful musical voice, speaking with the appropriate gravity, in a key and orchestration that finally links it with the theme's initial appearance in 1A. It is the last time that Richard's musical voice is given the limelight and distinguished from its associations with Robin and the love theme.

Example 5.4. Development of Last Phrase of Richard's Theme

Robin's heroic theme is first introduced in cue 1C as he and Will Scarlett ride into shot (see example 4.6) and is reprised in 1D.[10] It is also heard in the cues that quote directly from *Sursum Corda* (see chapter 4) and as Robin competes in the archery tournament disguised as a tinker. No disguise can match his prowess, though, and in cue 6D we hear his theme ring out in A-flat major to the evident concern of the watching Marian. In 1F, as Robin causes a scuffle outside Nottingham Castle's Great Hall, we hear the theme in its shortened 'head motif' form (see example 5.5). This consists of the opening fanfare at the fourth, followed by a number of seventh chords, which—with the rising minor ninth—suggest some link to Sir Guy's disjunct theme (see example 4.11). Indeed in contrast to the uncomplicated C-major diatonicism of the full theme's melody, this chromatic angst suggests something of Robin's complex character, a character that perhaps finds its closest parallel in Sir Guy.

This head motif—sometimes shortened even further to the fanfare itself, as at the end of cue 1D when Robin threatens Sir Guy with his bow—is used throughout the score in numerous guises to signal

Robin's presence. As Robin and Will make their escape in 2C, for example, the fanfare rings out over the rhythm of galloping horses and is answered by the disjunct chords. The head motif is also heard in 3E as Norman oppressors are punished by Robin's black arrows. Though we don't always see him in shot, it is therefore clear that the black arrows originate from his bow: in addition, the motif is precisely coordinated with the flight of the shots, thus identifying the arrows as projections of Robin's musical voice. Other uses of the head motif are heard when Robin is arrested and led away (7B and 7C), and as he is led to the gallows (7D, see example 5.6)

Example 5.5. Robin's Head Motif

The Jollity theme (see example 4.7) has no fixed associations and seems to stand for a sense of shared camaraderie. Yet, as demonstrated in chapter 4, its melody is also closely related to Robin's theme and thus bonds Robin to his fellow Merry Men. It first appears in cues 3B and 3C, as Robin meets and fights Little John, and reappears as Robin fights Friar Tuck (4A) in a longer version that anticipates its use in the attack on Sir Guy's treasure caravan (4C). As will become clear below, Robin's theme eventually develops in a way that distances itself slightly from "Jollity," as if his growing love for Marian and his restoration of rank at the end of the film removes him from the youthful comradely bond he enjoys with his band.

The love theme, too, is closely linked with both Robin's theme and "Jollity" (see examples 4.6–4.10), and—through its opening dotted rhythm—with the first bar of Richard's theme; yet, it too, is eventually distanced from "Jollity" and allied even more closely with Richard. It is first introduced in cue 5E, after a magical modulation to C major from the preceding D minor, as Robin and Marian leave the darkness of the forest and the suffering of the poor people. As there is little in the dialogue at this stage to indicate their growing love (Marian does claim that she begins "to see a little now," and Robin kisses her hand), it perhaps gains its associations retrospectively from the 'official' love scene (8B). Yet as part of a 1930s film music Text, or indeed a Korngoldian Text, it is obviously an archetypal love theme, particularly with its string textures and yearning rising fifth. Its next, and most dominant, appearance is in cue 8B where it is also heard along with the themes for Robin, Marian, and Richard and is firmly connected with the concept of love indicated in the dialogue.

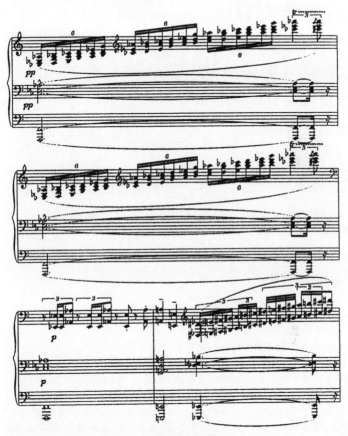

Example 5.6. Robin Is Led to the Gallows

While cue 5E first associated the love theme (and thus Robin's music) with Richard's and Marian's themes, it is 8B where thematic transformation begins to occur and we have a sense of the overall destination of the narrative. As Robin climbs the ivy to Marian's room in the castle, we hear the opening bars of his theme slightly altered over harp and flutter-tongue flute arpeggios. In this guise, it anticipates the transformation of his theme heard at the film's conclusion in cues 11D and 11E (see example 5.7). The theme abandons the disjunct quaver motion (A- D-G-E) of "Jollity," and it thus seems as if the love he feels for Marian takes him away from the comradely bond enjoyed by the group.[11]

(Robin's original theme—note disjunct quaver motion)

(Robin's theme slightly transformed in 8B)

(Robin's final theme in 11E)

Example 5.7. The Development of Robin's Theme

At the same time, Robin's theme is also more closely allied with King Richard's. In its transformed version in 11E, for example, the ending is characterized by the same descending scale found at the end of Richard's theme (see example 5.4). This occurs after Robin has asked the restored king for a pardon for his men and the hand of Marian, thus severing all his ties and obligations and establishing the new order. His transformed theme is also far nobler and stately than the impish heroic theme first associated with him in 1C. Robin's tasks (restoring Richard and winning the hand of Marian) are accomplished, he has been restored to rank, and his musical voice has changed as a result.

Similarly, the love theme itself is eventually altered to limit the disjunct movement of "Jollity" and Robin's original theme. In 11D, when Robin has rescued Marian, the second part of the phrase is miss-

ing and instead develops along different lines (example 5.8). Robin and
Marian's love is thus altered: it seems to have grown beyond the implications of the Jollity theme into something more distinct. And yet the
love theme continues in 11D with the same development of Richard's
theme heard in 10C (see example 5.4). While Robin's love for Marian
had always been associated with his love for England—via the rhythmic similarities in the two themes' openings, and the simultaneous
presence of the themes in 5E and 8B—the love theme in 11D is now
almost indistinguishable from Richard's theme. Robin's love for his
king and country and his love for Marian are thus united, separated
from the youthful exuberance and all-male company of "Jollity."

Example 5.8. The Love Theme in 11D

Marian

Marian's theme (see example 4.2) is instantly associated with her, as it
is first heard when she is introduced in cue 1E during the banquet at
Nottingham Castle. It follows on easily from the English Air theme
(see below), as if to emphasize that her loyalties initially lie with the
Normans; yet her theme is noticeably simpler with less chromatic embellishment, somehow more innocent and serene than the restless
chromaticism and mock pomposity of the Norman air that precedes it.
It is heard again in cue 5E, but receives its most interesting treatment in

cue 7C; here, it is first cast in B-flat minor and signals Robin's thoughts turning to Marian as he contemplates his fate in the dungeon. Then a sorrowful D-minor version is heard as we cut to her anxiously pulling leaves out of the ivy at her window. No dialogue is required to establish Marian's mood; it is evident in her *musical* voice. Bess (Marian's lady-in-waiting) has no musical voice of her own (though the Flirt theme discussed below functions as a parodic love theme for her and Much), and she can only talk in Marian's music: her mournful cor anglais thus echoes Marian's maidenly flute in sympathetic concern, as the music modulates to A-flat, offering a scrap of comfort to her mistress. As Marian begins to talk with words rather than music, we hear the last phrase of her theme in A-flat major, and the cue finishes while Marian and Bess are in mid-conversation. Indeed, this is one occasion where the resolution of the cue's end seems to bear no resemblance to the narrative content of the scene, which is still ongoing. Nevertheless, the resolution offered by the theme's modulation to a stable major key reveals to the audience that Bess's knowledge of the Merry Men's location will allow Marian to communicate to them the details of Robin's death sentence and thus save the day.

The last instance of Marian's theme occurs in the coda to the love scene (8B), where it is presented in its entirety and in its original G major, as she bids farewell to Robin. It is marked *dolcissimo* and is performed more slowly than its first appearance in 1E. This is the end of Marian's independence from Robin and, as such, represents a nostalgic, almost bittersweet, farewell to her own musical voice.

Sir Guy

Sir Guy's angular theme is characterized by rising major sevenths and minor ninths. It is first heard in cue 1C and initially functions as the dominant preparation for Robin's own entrance (see example 4.11), perhaps suggesting that these two seemingly opposing characters are, in fact, closely connected.

The theme returns in 1D as Robin and Sir Guy trade dialogue, and it features prominently at the end of cue 2B as Sir Guy berates his men for their failure to capture the outlaw. It can be heard with a stately accompaniment in cue 4C (the attack on the treasure caravan) as a sequence of serenely ascending major sevenths and appears in other cues when Sir Guy is in shot, for example, in 5D, 5E, the very beginning of 7A, and 11C.

Oppression

The theme associated with the Norman oppression is characterized by two semitones separated by a minor third (see example 5.9). It first appears in cue 1C during a montage of suffering Saxons and returns in the next montage sequence in 3E, seemingly functioning as the collective angry voice of the people. In 5E, as Robin shows Marian the victims of Prince John's reign of terror, the theme is fragmented over a tonic pedal in a slow funereal manner as if to show the effects of the terror and the resigned attitude of the people, rather than the oppression itself. In 6E, however, it is combined with a muted trumpet intoning Robin's fanfare head motif: clearly, he is the victim on this occasion. Similarly, as Robin is put on trial and led away to the dungeon in cues 7B and 7C, it appears slightly altered rhythmically, with the fanfare of Robin's head motif in timpani. Evidently, this theme is connected with the concept of oppression and can be invoked by any of the characters, no matter what their social rank. Thus when Marian herself is arrested (9A) we also hear it in its original 1C form. The shock at seeing Marian, the royal ward, subjected to the same treatment as the Saxon peasants is thus reflected in a shared musical voice: the rejection of her own Norman background and acceptance of her new national status and shared sense of suffering thus allies Marian with the Saxons.

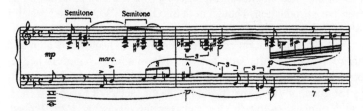

Example 5.9. Oppression Theme

Other Themes

Prince John's theme is the fanfare that is heard at the end of 1A as the narrative intertitle references his plans. As discussed below, its narrative status is always in doubt, however, and it frequently seems to cross the boundaries between the diegetic and nondiegetic. It returns in 1B, and again in 1E as one of his knights offers him a toast (see example 5.10.), but receives its most extensive treatment in the tournament sequence (cues 6A–6E), where it is slightly altered. The fanfare then returns in its original form in cue 11A as Prince John processes toward his coronation.

Example 5.10. Prince John's Fanfare

The theme associated with the horses is a compound duple rhythm, and is perhaps more correctly labeled as a topic. It is first introduced in 1C as Much is chased by Norman horses and is much like material used in *Another Dawn* when Denny and his men engage the Arabs or in *The Prince and the Pauper* when soldiers appear on horseback accompanying the king's messenger. Raymond Monelle argues that this topic—most famously used in "The Ride of the Valkyries" from Wagner's *Die Walküre*—is largely confined to music of the period after about 1800, though he cites earlier appearances in Monteverdi.[12] He also points out that the use of an equestrian topic in music also makes reference to the past, to "medieval, legendary, or fictional times," and carries noble and military associations.[13] Example 5.11 shows its use in cue 2C.

Having 'welcomed' Sir Guy and his party to Sherwood, Robin leads them to his camp accompanied by an E-flat-major theme labeled "Flirt" in the piano-conductor score (see example 5.12), preceded by an eleven-bar introduction. Though both Sir Guy and Will Scarlett are also in shot, it seems possible that this elegant and noble melody with its aristocratic ornamentation could be a proto-love theme for Robin and Marian. While he flirts with her, she labels him a charmless hedge-robber, to the amusement of Will. At the same time, however, the melody also functions as a love theme for the characters of Much and Bess, a comic romance to parallel that between the main characters. Indeed, the exchange between Much and Bess is longer and features a new phrase on solo violin that is so sugary sweet, it is almost kitsch. This, then, is flirtatious music, a comic parody and prelude to the love theme itself. The theme is transformed into a waltz in 5B and is heard in its original form in 5C as Robin continues to flirt with Marian. It returns finally at the end of 5E: Much copies Robin's lead by offering his arm to Bess, and she and Marian are escorted homeward. The theme thus has no fixed associations with characters, but serves to emphasize the comic parallels between the two romances.

Example 5.11. The Horse Topic in 2C

Example 5.12. "Flirt" in 5A

The English Air theme (see example 5.13) is heard only during the banquet at Nottingham Castle (1E) and is typical of Korngold's evocations of domesticity.[14] The melody is simple, though the harmony possesses a certain amount of pompous chromatic embellishment, and is dominated texturally by the trumpet and strings. It perhaps serves as the musical equivalent of the sense of security and comfort enjoyed by the Normans: as such, it seems appropriate that it should not return in the rest of the film, since Robin has the Normans very much on the run. During Prince John's dialogue, the melody is varied with a more intimate orchestration for flutes and clarinets, emphasizing his effete characterization.[15] Thus, behind the public façade of Prince John's masculine fanfare lies a more delicate, more effeminate musical voice.

Example 5.13. The English Air Theme

Friar Tuck's theme (see example 5.14) is also confined to a small part of the score, namely, cues 3F and 4A. It is first intoned in cellos—over which flutes, a solo violin, vibraphone, and celesta sparkle magically—and is appropriately marked "*poco religioso*." It is characterized by a relatively simple diatonicism and a gentleness that belies Tuck's combative nature. As a result, it seems to reflect Robin's naïve conception of the friar's character, rather than representing Tuck's own musical voice.[16] Similarly, Hugo Friedhofer orchestrates one of the phrases of the theme with an alto saxophone to signify Tuck's earthy appetites. Here, then, is the composer/orchestrator apparently adopting a narrating voice, reading the character and encoding him for the audience to recognize. Never, it seems, do we hear Tuck's own musical voice speaking; rather, he seems to subsume himself as part of the collective and is thus associated more with the March and "Jollity."

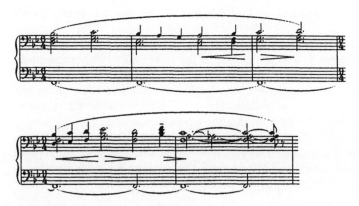

Example 5.14. Friar Tuck's Theme

Demarcation and Subversion of Narrative Space

Korngold's treatment of narrative space is, as acknowledged in chapter 2, one of his trademarks. While his music in *The Adventures of Robin Hood* outlines spatial relationships between characters and locations, and contributes to the construction of the narrative through mickey-mousing, it also subverts the boundaries between the diegetic and non-diegetic, thereby creating extra levels of sophistication.

The horse topic, for example, is often used to support the illusion of three-dimensional space on the two-dimensional screen: at the end of 2C a hesitant *piano* statement is heard ascending in pitch as the Normans recede into the distance, chasing Robin and Will's riderless horses. Similarly, cross-cutting between different locales is matched by sudden changes in musical content. At the beginning of the tournament scene (cue 6A), for example, Korngold synchronizes a number of three-bar phrases—each based on an unrelated chord (B-flat^7; F-sharp^7; E-flat^7)—with a change of shot (the archery field; Prince John, Sir Guy, and Marian; the archery field with pennants in the foreground). Likewise in 3B, where Robin first meets Little John, the change of camera angle to show Little John's easy stroll is matched by a modulation from D to G major; as Robin approaches, the key shifts again, to F major. Even when the camerawork seems more fluid, Korngold can use thematicism to make clear distinctions between different character relationships and their spatial positions: when Robin and Marian return after their excursion to visit the poor people (cue 5E), references to

Marian's theme and Sir Guy's own theme are heard in quick succession.

One of the film's standout set pieces, the attack on Sir Guy's treasure caravan, is also a highlight of the score in its synchronization of music and picture, its integration of thematicism, and its subsequent delineation of narrative space. Table 5.1 summarizes the visual and musical structure of the cue. The cross-cutting between the scenes of Robin and his men engaging the advance guard and Sir Guy's party riding toward the trap are thus perfectly matched by the musical structure of the sequence. The moment when the Sheriff of Nottingham spies the attack and brings these two separate locations together is achieved effortlessly by the score (see example 5.15).

Table 5.1. Cue 4C

Bar	Timing	Visuals	Music
1	0:33:23	Preparations of Merry Men.	B-flat-major orchestration of the March of the Merry Men.
18.4	0:34:16	Long shot of Sir Guy's party. Much spots them, as does Little John.	Leaping minor 9ths in violins.
46	0:34:39	Close up of Sheriff, Sir Guy, and Marian. Dialogue.	Sir Guy's theme in muted trumpets (rising major 7ths) with B-flat-minor coloring.
62	0:35:01	Robin and his men observe the approaching party.	March of the Merry Men in C major with excited triplets in cellos. March fragments into shorter phrases.
85.3	0:35:42	Will informs Robin that Sir Guy and the sheriff have stopped. Robin hands out his orders.	Music stops on *tremolando* octave D, which ascends chromatically as fragments of the march are tossed about at different registers in response to Robin's orders.
96	0:36:00	Long shot of horses drinking. Shots of men waiting to ambush the advance guard.	*Poco sostenuto, misterioso* 2/2. Sequentially repeated four-bar phrase based on a phrase of the march with a crescendo at the end. The last six bars are synchronized with six changes of camera shot.
107	0:36:17	Men jumping out of trees and attacking.	Runs and busy semiquaver activity.

Table 5.1. Cue 4C (continued)

Bar	Timing	Visuals	Music
121	0:36:37 ·	Sir Guy's party advancing stately.	Sir Guy's theme; return to the march accompaniment.
125	0:36:43	Attack continues.	Semiquaver activity.
130	0:36:49	Sir Guy's party.	Sir Guy's theme and march accompaniment.
136	0:36:58	Attack continues; Sheriff spots the trouble.	Activity with offbeat *sforzando* chords (see example 5.15).
140	0:37:03	Men jump out of trees; attack ends. Robin swings in on vine to land atop a rock; he welcomes Marian.	Jollity theme in F major, much like cue 4A. Modulates to A major. Cue ends with Robin's head motif passed around, a swirling glissando down and back up, and a final statement of the head motif in A major.

Sometimes the spatial outlining achieved by the music can fool us into expecting a change of shot. In cue 3D, as word of a meeting in Sherwood is spread, Robin's head motif is heard with a rocking harp and celesta accompaniment over a series of chords held in flutes and strings. The ascending pattern of chords (B-flat minor, C-sharp minor, F major) seems to mirror the intensification of the message's import, as more of the Saxons are informed of the meeting, yet the shifts in chord are not always precisely timed to the visual cuts, and there are more 'locations' than chords. Here, then, the music is outlining spatial relationships that are not suggested by the images.

The score's close synchronization with images is also manifested in mickey-mousing, a feature of classical film-scoring technique commonly associated with Max Steiner. In 7A, for instance, a captured Robin is brought before Sir Guy and given a xylophone slap across the face, while in 1C the dripping red wine (overtly symbolizing the spilled blood of the Saxons) is matched by the chromatic descent of the bass clarinet and cellos. Likewise, the clashes of quarterstaffs as Robin and Little John fight are coordinated with pizzicato chords (cue 3B), while the sound of an arrow in flight is augmented throughout the score by grace notes (see example 5.16). Leaps and falls are also given the full mickey-mouse treatment: Much ambushes Dickon to a harp and violin glissando in 10A; Sir Guy's death and fall from a great height is accompanied by a passage marked "*precipitando*"; Robin's fall into the river in 3C (his fight with Little John) prompts a downward scale; and

Tuck's comic head-first tumble into the water is matched by a mickey-mouse run in strings, clarinets, and bassoons and a harp glissando.

Example 5.15. The Sheriff Spies the Attack

Example 5.16. Arrows (From Opening of 8A)

One of the most interesting characteristics of the score, though, is the way it subverts the idea of narrative boundaries between the diegetic and nondiegetic—how the score both inhabits the diegetic space of the narrative and stands apart as a narrating voice. To some extent, the discussion of thematic voices offered above implies that the score literally inhabits the fairy-tale world of the characters. This, after all, is a highly mythologized reality, and it must be entertained that the characters potentially hear their musical voices as clearly as their spoken ones. Similarly, the score can imitate the sounds of nature: in cue 3B when Robin talks of "nightingales singing," a solo violin glissandos repeatedly to a harmonic A almost in imitation of birdsong. Again, we might wonder whether, in this mythologized world, birds actually do sing like violins.

While the terms *diegetic* and *nondiegetic* are used throughout film musicology to identify the narrative status of music, they are, as many have recognized, problematic.[17] Kassabian asks whether the distinction obscures music's role in producing the diegesis itself—whether music can *ever* be really nondiegetic.[18] The dichotomy also suggests that music can be categorized as either 'in or out' of the diegesis. Clearly there are instances where music falls between these poles, where its status is ambiguous. Can the characters hear it? Do they hear the same music as the audience? Filmmakers can, of course, play with the conventions that assume orchestral underscore to be nondiegetic. In *The Truman Show* (1998), for instance, music plays a primary role in blurring the boundaries between 'reality' and the illusory reality of Truman's world, creating worlds within worlds; music that we might initially assume to be entirely nondiegetic is sometimes revealed to be nondiegetic only to Truman and is heard by the internal audience of the film.

The opening of *The Adventures of Robin Hood* also blurs boundaries and suggests that the distinction between diegetic and nondiegetic is an oversimplification. As the second page of narration fades out, the opening cue of the film (comprising the March and Richard's theme) continues with Prince John's fanfare. Then something quite magical happens: the first scene of the film fades in, and we see two drummers on horseback playing in perfect synchronization with the timpani. The fanfare thus seems to inhabit the narrative world of the film; the trumpeters, we assume, are out of shot somewhere. Do the characters gathered in the town square hear the trumpeters and drums? It would seem so; have they also heard the march that preceded it, though? That question is not so easy to answer. The very next cue is a muted version of Prince John's fanfare, as if heard from a distance, and gives the impression that Prince John and Sir Guy have been listening to the messenger's speech—and the diegetic fanfares—from Nottingham Castle. The talk between Sir Guy and Prince John is of the news delivered by the messenger and the Saxons' reaction to it. The score thus cleverly outlines a spatial and hierarchical relationship between the town and its

people on the one hand and the lofty removed world of Sir Guy and
Prince John on the other.

In fact, much of the music that surrounds the Normans could be labeled "quasi-diegetic." In the banquet scene in the Great Hall (cue 1E),
diegetic musicians are in shot (though they look more like statues than
performers, further confusing their narrative status). If they are playing,
though, at what point in the cue does the music cease to be diegetic? Do
the on-screen musicians play Marian's theme at the end of the cue?
Similarly, in the tournament scene (cues 6A–6E), the fanfares could be
labeled diegetic at some points—since we see trumpeters with raised
instruments—but are the fanfares throughout the rest of the sequence
fully diegetic? Since the music consists of a variant of Prince John's
theme, it seems entirely appropriate to the occasion. What of the rest of
the orchestra, though? With the fairy-tale look and feel of the film at
this point, there is perhaps no need to appeal to verisimilitude. The visual presence of other instrumentalists is not required for us to believe
that this music is somehow 'heard' by the characters.

The coronation scene at the film's climax (cues 10E and 11A)
likewise contains some moments that are difficult to categorize as either 'in' or 'out' of the diegesis. As the scene shifts to the castle interior
and Prince John's preparations for the ceremony, a ceremonial F-sharp
chime and tam-tam peal is heard in the score for two bars, joined by
celesta runs, harps, and glockenspiel in B major. At this moment, the
music seems to cross the boundaries of the diegesis, and Sir Guy,
Prince John, and the Sheriff look around suddenly in response; the
Sheriff, having heard the bells, announces that the ceremony is ready to
begin. As the procession of the disguised Merry Men enters the Great
Hall, diegetic trumpeters raise their instruments to play fanfares. These
same instrumentalists 'play' more fanfares at the start of 11A, before
Prince John's theme is heard three times on stopped horns and, later,
muted trumpets, alternating with material derived from the March of
the Merry Men.[19] Are John's fanfares played by the same diegetic
trumpeters? and, if so, who is playing the March, and why? The
boundaries between diegetic and nondiegetic music are well and truly
scrambled throughout this processional sequence. The March seems
entirely appropriate as ceremonial music, and yet only the trumpeters
are visible. In addition, for Sir Guy's musicians to perform with the
musical voice of his sworn enemy would be unthinkable; rather, this
might be seen as the true musical voice of the disguised Merry Men
leaking into the diegesis, played not by any on-screen instrumentalists
but existing intrinsically in the mythologized world of the narrative.

At times, the music also appears to be controlled directly by the characters, as if they are manipulating the underscore. At the end of cue 3C, in response to the diegetic chords of Will Scarlett's lute-like instrument, Little John calls out, "Hey there pretty fellow, play a livelier tune that I can make this puny rascal [Robin] dance to." Will responds to Little John's challenge, and a speeded-up version of "Jollity" is heard in the underscore, but it seems to be Robin who is in charge of the music, responding to Little John's taunt with, "You need a merrier tune? Well how's this?!" Little John's victory, however, seems to wrest control of the music, and his laughter is reinforced by mocking woodwinds.

At other times, though, the underscore does appear to act as a narrating voice and to be entirely nondiegetic. Little John's woodwind laughter could, in fact, be the laughter of this nondiegetic narrating voice; when Friar Tuck suffers a similar wetting in 4A, the woodwind laughter returns. Earlier in the same cue, despite the fury on Robin's face as he is almost bested by the swordsmanship of Tuck, the music remains entirely good natured, reassuring the viewer that—like Little John before him—Tuck will eventually fall into line. Only with the omniscience of a narrating voice can this interpretation be entertained.

This subversion of the unambiguously nondiegetic narrative status of the underscore is done particularly skillfully. When combined with the arguably masterful way in which music delineates spatial relationships and the way in which the thematic structure contributes to the narrative, it becomes relatively straightforward to see why this score could be said to have provided other composers with a model of film music aesthetics. In other words, the score seems to communicate at a universal level, to provide a blueprint for the classical Hollywood score. And yet, there are other elements of the score's meaning that rely far more on intertextual references, many of which may not be immediately apparent to the audience. While many of the 'conventions' outlined above are reliant on the existence of other musical or film score Texts—the appropriateness of thematic ideas, or the assumed nondiegetic status of the score, for example—we can also examine the effect of other Texts on the meanings an audience member might read into this score.

Meaning and Intertextuality in *Robin Hood*

Before other possible readings are examined, let us begin with perhaps the most interesting of these intertextual references, the quotations from *Sursum Corda* and *Rosen aus Florida*. Both of these are intimately connected with Korngold's musical past in Vienna, and their use can therefore be read within the context of the contemporary political situation. While Korngold's perceived political naïveté has been noted, he was working on the score while anxiously waiting for news of his family, aware that his property was being seized by the Nazis. It is not surprising that the score can be read, then, as embodying a musical idealization of Austrian life, a nostalgic testament to Korngold's own musical heritage.

As part of a beauty contest of nations in *Rosen aus Florida*, "Miß Austria" is Korngold's attempt at summarizing the musical features of his homeland. Although doubtless an affectionate parody of the Austrian love for the waltz (the onstage "Miß Austria" is preceded by a violinist in traditional Viennese costume), it nevertheless encodes Austrian-ness, and specifically a Viennese Austrian-ness, in music. Though Korngold initially disguises this waltz as the March of the Merry Men, he introduces it in the opening notes of the score. Furthermore, the very first line of dialogue is "News has come from Vienna." For the 1938 audience, bad news had indeed come from Vienna just a couple of months before the film opened (the Anschluss). Immediately then, the fairy-tale nature of the presentation, and the disguise of the score, seems to camouflage the enormous contemporary relevance of the film. "Miß Austria" is not revealed in its original waltz form until cue 5B, as we see scenes of food being prepared for the feast in Sherwood. As the most overt reference to Austria in the score, this scene is very much, as many have quipped, "Robin Hood in the Vienna Woods." This picture of nature and good food is perhaps Korngold's idealized, nostalgic view of Austrian life, the "heaven" that Robin proclaims Sherwood at this moment to be. Similarly, the first four notes of the theme for Richard/England (see example 5.2) outline the same opening intervals found in the Mahler song "Das himmlische Leben" (The Heavenly Life) from *Des Knaben Wunderhorn*.[20]

Robin's entrance in cue 1C prompts the first musical remembrance of *Sursum Corda*. Its links to the Vienna of Korngold's early adulthood also suggest that a nostalgic Vienna itself, embodied in Robin, is riding to the rescue of the oppressed Much. Similarly, the use of a section from *Sursum Corda* as a love theme can be read as an expression of national love. As we have discovered, the scenes where it is used (5E, 8B, 11D) also make reference to a loyalty for a deposed sovereign and a love for one's country. While contemporary Vienna was riddled with anti-Semitism, this nod to Korngold's musical past can be seen as an appeal to a time that must have seemed more stable to the composer, and even as an expression of loyalty to the deposed Schuschnigg, for all his faults. Ironically, in its dedication to Richard Strauss—a figure whose stance towards the Nazis has been somewhat controversial— *Sursum Corda* also speaks of the complexities of the political situation.

Similarly, the religious overtones of the work's title hint at the religious conflicts embodied in both the various treatments of the Robin Hood legend and in contemporary anti-Semitism.[21] Indeed, while *Ivanhoe* tackles the anti-Semitism of the twelfth century, *The Adventures of Robin Hood* avoids it, yet firmly allies the Norman oppressors with the high church of the Bishop of the Black Canons. After Robin's escape from Nottingham Castle, for instance, we see the shadow of a dead Norman laid out in a typically distinctive piece of Sol Polito cinematography and also hear the sound of a priest intoning a Requiem Mass. The connection between the oppression represented by the Normans and the Latin church, and its contrast with the liberal, yet pious, practices of Friar Tuck, Robin, and Marian (who swears by "our Lady" to help Robin) is thus further emphasized.

The continued references to *Sursum Corda*, once recognized, therefore continually remind the audience of political situations in twentieth-century Austria and twelfth-century England. However, the transformations and developments of the themes for both Robin and Richard, and their frequent proximity to each other, mean that contemporary America is also referenced, as noted in Ina Rae Hark's article on the film (see chapter 3). By combining Richard's and Robin's themes in cue 10B, for example, and ultimately developing Robin's theme along the same line as Richard's, the score contributes to a reading of the film that sees these two characters as allegories of Franklin D. Roosevelt. While the thematic alignment of these characters makes sense without this knowledge, Hark's assertion that Richard, Robin, and Roosevelt are linked adds intertextual meaning to this musical process.

The Self-Other dualities that are arguably inherent in Western thought also find expression in the score, though a reading that acknowledges their presence is intertextually dependent on the thinking of Edward Said and others.[22] The conflict between the Normans and Saxons, for example, is encoded in a dichotomy between chromaticism and diatonicism. Sir Guy's theme, with its major sevenths and minor ninths, and the Oppression theme form part of this Norman Otherness, while Sir Guy and Prince John scheme in 6E to rising chromatic lines. It is perhaps most clear, though, in the modernist textures of the knife fight (9B and 10A). This fight between Much and Dickon is no noble duel, like that between Robin and Sir Guy, but a visceral death struggle. As such, it also suggests a class struggle in which Much and Dickon (as the peasant and disgraced nobleman) are Othered from the higher normative social world of Sir Guy and Robin (despite his temporary departure from rank). It is characterized by a musical language based on superimposed minor seconds (see example 5.17). The orchestration is also particularly arresting: *ponticello tremelando* strings, celesta, vibraphone, and muted flutter-tongue trumpets combine to create a musical world entirely removed from the safe diatonic romanticism of our heroes.

On the other side, then, the normative world of Robin Hood mythology is characterized by diatonic melodies that are merely colored by chromaticism (for there is always something desired in that which is Othered). The juxtaposition between these two basic musical languages can be clearly seen in cue 3F. Sir Guy has just vowed to deal with Robin upon his return from Kenworth Castle when one of Robin's black arrows, accompanied by his head motif, impales the table in front of him. The dissolve from this scene into the next set piece of Robin Hood mythology, the encounter with the Curtal Friar, is made via a chord marked *misterioso* in the full score. This chord is made up of three superimposed diminished sevenths, though the descending bass misses out the G: thus only one of the twelve chromatic pitches is absent from this chord. Nevertheless, it has a tonal function, with the upper note, A, leading to the uncomplicated 2nd inversion B-flat major chord as Friar Tuck's fish appears in shot (see example 5.18). The relatively simple diatonicism thus contrasts with the previously chromatically saturated angst of the Normans and the important narrative information detailed in the previous scene. Thus our retreat back into the mythology of Robin Hood, rather than the modernist narrative devised by the scriptwriters of 1937, signals a return to uncomplicated diatonicism.

Similarly, a Self-Other duality can be found in a gendered reading of parts of the score. The encoding of Prince John's effete characterization in the woodwind orchestration of 1E has already been mentioned, and other examples of this gender coding can be found throughout the score. These associations of gender with particular instrumental combinations (woodwind and strings as feminine; brass and percussion as masculine) are clearly created intertextually. Thus in cue 3B, when Little John questions Robin's masculinity, Robin goes off to fetch a quarterstaff to a determined D-major statement of "Jollity" in horns, with strong off-beat pizzicatos in strings, as if to establish his masculinity in contrast with the earlier woodwind- and harp-dominated texture. Indeed, we could suggest that it was this 'feminized' musical characterization that prompted Little John to question Robin's masculinity in the first place. Similarly Marian is nearly always voiced by violins or woodwind, while Friar Tuck, for example, finds his musical voice in the bassoon.

Example 5.17. The Knife Fight

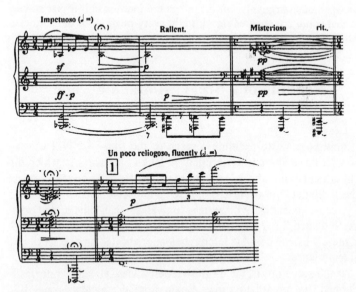

Example 5.18. The Opening of Cue 3F

Other, perhaps more intentional, intertextual meanings can be found in Korngold's nostalgic evocation of the film's English setting. Thus Little John whistles the thirteenth-century tune "Summer Is Icumen In" in 3B, while both the Old English Air of cue 1E and Marian's theme were undoubtedly influenced by Korngold's investigation of ballad tunes of the sixteenth and seventeenth centuries. They both share suitably archaic rhythmic patterns and phraseology and can thus be seen as a reference to some ideal 'Englishness' that is musically Elizabethan. These intertextual meanings are arguably recognizable to a much wider spectrum of people than the references to Korngold's Viennese past. Like the appropriateness of the thematic material, or the existence of a horse topic, this evocation of an idealized England is therefore dependent on other Texts, namely, a country's national traditions. Indeed, while the majority of the audience would not recognize the specific references to Korngold's Viennese past, they might conceivably identify the Sherwood banquet waltz with the stylized waltzes found in Lehár's operettas or the output of the Strauss family. Thus the tension between meaning that is 'universal' and understood by all because it appears intrinsic to the Text, and that which is specific to the individual reader and predicated on the idea of Intertext is, in many ways, specious. Arguably, *all* meanings are intertextual; it just so happens that some are apparent to virtually every member of the audience, and thus approach the level of a universally understood convention.

Reading of a Scene: Robin's Escape from the Gallows

It is now possible to examine a scene of the film—we will use cue 8A—with these approaches in mind: to look at the ways in which different critical and authorial voices are woven together by the presence of the individual viewer/listener to create the score's meaning. Necessarily, some meanings will be less 'universal' than others, and some more 'intended,' and the following reading must therefore be considered merely as one possible interpretation, predicated on one set of musical experiences.

As the scene opens, the disguised Merry Men, already strategically positioned, are poised to spring Robin from the gallows rope; Will Scarlett whispers "Get ready," and the cue begins (67:06). It opens with a drum roll, suggesting expectation, tension, and the possibility of a (literally) death-defying stunt (due to its intertextual connections with the drum roll heard before the fall of the guillotine or a dangerous circus trick). Arrows fly through the air synchronized with grace-note strings and Robin's head motif (67:08), and the harmony outlines a spatial and sequential relationship: the guards must be shot in sequence, it seems. The fanfares of Robin's head motif further reinforce the intertextual reference to the circus, while Robin's theme itself also references military traditions of music: Robin is portrayed in the manner of a commanding officer whose ability is rewarded by the loyalty of his men; throughout the film, he is unquestioningly a master tactician (until undone by love for Marian) and a fighter.

A scream (67:11), indicating terror, separates the fanfares from a series of chords with violent overtones (because of their similarity to the opening of cue 2B in which Robin escapes from Nottingham Castle amid scenes of violence). Although Robin's fate remains in question, the perfect cadence in C (67:14) provides a temporary sense of resolution. The score begins its quotation from *Sursum Corda*, reinforcing the link between the character of Robin and the optimistic, pious tone of the work's title (and its programmatic sense of struggle) and suggesting that a nostalgic Austria is once again coming to the rescue. Yet, by this point in the film, this simple association has been subverted: in cue 7A, Robin was captured to the same heroic theme, and the music does not therefore guarantee success.

The shot of Marian and her concerned look is accompanied by a German augmented sixth chord (67:24). A smile also plays on the corners of her mouth, suggesting a repressed joy that is checked by both her concern for Robin's safety and her own delicate position in the 'enemy camp.' The momentary turn to an augmented sixth chord, and nervous repetition, suggests a deviation from the simple, uncomplicated heroism of the C-major main theme, and thus symbolizes Marian's concern and uncertainty, while the leaping seventh interval to the top D is simultaneously indicative of her hope. The chord can also be interpreted as a flattened submediant seventh chord, a harmonic area that, in Schubert, has sometimes been associated with the romantic concept of distance.[23] Marian, it seems, is separated from Robin, yet intrinsically linked with his fate.

As the music begins to modulate to E major (67:36), knowledge of *Sursum Corda* will suggest to the informed listener that two bars are 'missing' (see chapter 4), since they exist in another version of the music; as the sequence approaches, a question thus arises: will the score restore the missing bars? At these points, the listener is perhaps aligned with the composer and orchestrator, who would undoubtedly experience a similar reaction. This could be characterized as a moment of particular 'intertextual instability.'[24] Robin has been out of shot for a while, and the audience perhaps wonders where he is. The cadence in E major (67:40) reestablishes harmonic and intertextual stability (8A and *Sursum Corda* are back on track) and coincides with a shot of Robin and his Merry Men.

Friar Tuck's mobile barrier slows the chasing Normans: the rhythmic movement lengthens from crotchets to triplet minims to a semibreve with a pause, while the splintering of wood is blended with a cymbal roll and harp glissando in mickey-mouse fashion. At this point (67:51), another moment of intertextual instability occurs. *Sursum Corda*, the radio version of the cue, and the trailer music (see chapter 4) proceed in a different manner, while 'new' material is introduced in the film (see example 5.19).

(Figure 8 Film Version)

(Trailer and Radio Version)
Example 5.19. Intertextual Instability at Figure 8

The portcullis of Nottingham gate is open, symbolizing the freedom that awaits Robin and his men. Meanwhile, the melody in bassoons, violas, and cellos is a quicker version of the opening to cue 2A, Robin's entrance to Nottingham Castle. The same music thus accompanies Robin's voluntary and defiant entrance into enemy territory and his rather more hasty retreat. The advancing guard is surprised by a disguised member of Robin's band who throws a bucket of water over him, synchronized with a mickey-mouse harp 'splash.' The freedom

represented by the open gate in shot beckons (68:03) and we hear cele-
bratory bell-like tones in the music (piccolo, flute, piano, and strings),
again taken from *Sursum Corda*.

The musical movement slows down as the harmonic rhythms
lengthen; there is a fall in the bass line, from F to E-flat, and harmonic
stasis. At the same time, Robin halts his horse and remains on the camera's side of the gate. His severing of the rope holding the portcullis is
synchronized with syncopated chords in the music (68:18). Robin's
movements thus seem intrinsically musical, an interpretation further
reinforced by the mickey-mouse rising melodic figure in clarinets,
completed by flutes and piccolo, which matches his ascent. This is one
of the film's headline stunts, and we become particularly aware of the
film's status as a constructed diegesis at this point; in other words, an
appreciation of the film's production processes takes us out of the diegesis and bonds us to our fellow audience members.[25] The descent of
the portcullis, and the diegetic crash as it reaches the ground (68:25), is
synchronized by glissandi in harps and a downward movement in clarinets and violas. The contrast between the descending portcullis and the
ascending Robin also reflects the antithesis between good and evil: the
portcullis, symbol of Norman oppression, contrasts with Robin's heroic
status as defender and liberator of the people, and his ascent to the music of *Sursum Corda* has religious overtones.

Little John appears at the now-closed portcullis (68:33). Evidently
confused at Robin's absence and concerned for his safety, he asks,
"Robin, where are you?" Alan Hale (Little John) is a constant companion of Errol Flynn (Robin Hood) in many Warner Bros. films of the
period (see chapter 3). Their temporary separation seems to be given
added poignancy by this intertextual reference while the music's stasis
and repetition seem to echo the stasis in the narrative: Little John has
halted his own escape and returned to find Robin. His concern is synchronized with the syncopation and swells in piano and strings, while
the subject of his concern is indicated by the fragments of Robin's
theme in the bass. Robin asserts his authority with the order, "Here I
am...Stand by," while the music ascends in pitch as the camera pans
up, reflecting Robin's loftier position physically and authoritatively.

The appearance of the Normans on horseback (68:41) prompts an
appearance of the horse topic in the music. Its ascending character prepares for the musical descent of the violin and celesta line, matching
Robin's physical climb down the rope (68:43), while 1st trumpet and
trombones also provide small fanfare fragments that are part of Robin's
theme. The harmony consists of a series of unrelated chords strung to-

gether in a descending repeated sequence of roots: C major—G-flat major (down an augmented fourth)—E major (down a tone)—D major (down a tone)—E minor—B-flat major (down an augmented fourth)—A-flat major (down a tone)—G-flat major (down a tone)—A major—E-flat major (down an augmented fourth)—D-flat major (down a tone)—B major (down a tone), with the bass line: E—D-flat—B—A—G—F—E-flat—D-flat—C-sharp—B-flat—A-flat—F-sharp. The top line of the triads almost results in a descending whole-tone scale and therefore feels tonally unstable. Reference might be made to the descent of the rope in Prokofiev's *Peter and the Wolf* (1936), which has a similar sense of instability.[26] After Robin drops from the rope and hits the ground, stability is reasserted by the bass line. It settles on an A and returns to that pitch at the beginning of each of the next six bars. The references to Robin's theme continue with the fanfare fragments, and it is clear that the vast majority of the cue is centered on Robin, further cementing the link between the fanfare and his character.

The closed gate is in shot (68:55); however, this time the camera is on the other side and we hear (perhaps more than we see) the approaching horses in the music and sound effects. Success for Robin appears to be guaranteed, as there is now a clear barrier separating him from his pursuers. Robin and his men appear in shot, and their success is confirmed. The rising trajectory of the horse topic in the music synchronizes with the horses climbing the hill in the distance, while the orchestration is reduced and the music becomes quieter, thus outlining a spatial relationship between the camera and the characters: the music appears to emanate from Robin, his men, and their horses. The sound of Robin's horses galloping on grass also contrasts with the clattering of Norman horses on cobblestones. It is clear that Robin and his men have been reunited with the natural world and escaped the threat to 'England' that exists in the town.

The final B-major fragment of Robin's fanfare (69:04), as discussed in chapter 4, was only one of three possible endings to the cue, again creating a particularly overt intertextual instability. Although the cue ends here, there is no perfect cadence, merely an alternation between B major and G-sharp minor chords that feels almost like a plagal cadence (with the subdominant chord missing its root and gaining a major seventh). This, along with the diminuendo of the last chord and the fade to black, avoids any definitive conclusion and aids the link into the next scene, while maintaining a suitably final end to the sequence. The fanfare in brass also properly answers the drum roll from the beginning of the cue: the death-defying stunt is over and was successful;

Robin's military authority is restored. Coming after the disappearance of the Merry Men and their horses, the fanfare also seems to reassert the voice of a narrator, as if to announce the end of this staple set piece in the swashbuckler genre. The details of the escape arguably have little to do with the narrative in this particular film, and its successful conclusion is both expected by the audience (though Robin's earlier capture plays with these expectations) and demanded by the drum roll that begins the cue.

In common with discussions of intertextuality that stress its ability to disrupt the linear flow of history,[27] we can also make reference to a text that postdates 1938, namely, Ron Goodwin's score to the 1969 film *Battle of Britain*. The theme for the Royal Air Force in this film is fanfare-like and therefore alludes to Robin's theme, drawing on the same heroic associations; however, there is one point where the combination of rhythm, melody, and harmony is similar, in gestural terms at least, to 8A's ending. It is found at 1:45:43–1:45:47 on the region 2 DVD of the film.[28] An even closer reference might also be found in bars 195–197 of Wagner's overture to *Der fliegende Holländer*, where there is an almost identical fanfare, or in the introductory scene where the chorus of sailors sing the same music. Cue 8A's fanfare at the fourth, with alternating tonic and quasi-subdominant chords, thus brings Wagnerian associations.

Interestingly, *Der fliegende Holländer* is, after *Tannhäuser*, the music drama that Wagner revised the most; similarly, with three possible endings, 8A stands out as the most revised portion of *The Adventures of Robin Hood*. Its intertextual reference to Wagner ironically also brings us back to the notion of convention, the romantic aesthetic, and the ways in which classical-era Hollywood scores have been linked with concepts of leitmotiv and the Wagnerian idea of the *Gesamtkunstwerk* in order to elevate them culturally. By alluding to Wagner, the score reminds us of some of the questions that we have been concerned with throughout this volume: (1) How does this appeal to a romantic aesthetic of composition cloud our understanding of the way in which film scores were produced in the studio era? (2) How might we open up the question of a score's meaning by rejecting that same romantic aesthetic? (3) How does this affect our view of Korngold as 'composer' and the notion that he established a model of film scoring for others to follow?

Conclusion

As we have discovered with *The Adventures of Robin Hood*, film scores in the late 1930s are not the product of a single individual. Leaving aside their reliance on the visual aspect of film (the product of numerous collaborators), we can trace the authorial voices of orchestrators, music directors, and producers (to a greater or lesser extent) in addition to the composer's. Nor, as we have discovered with Korngold, is the composer's voice a unitary one-dimensional phenomenon: it can be a rich tapestry of voices, a vessel through which other composers or musical traditions can speak, where the composer's own past voices can make themselves heard. The composer, like the audience, is the 'ultimate' pluralistic Text, the 'I' of the viewing subject.

Similarly, the film score cannot be seen as a unitary aesthetic object: like *Der fliegende Holländer*, it may exist in numerous versions, each of which has value and might affect the way in which a score is read. By embracing 'Text' as a replacement conceptual framework for understanding the notion of 'a work' or 'a composer,' we have also opened up the possibility of much wider interpretative strategies for reading the film score. The intertextual references that occur to an audience become just as meaningful in unpicking a score's meanings as the intentions of a composer and allow the film score to be a living entity, continually reengaging with an audience's musical experiences (be they individual or shared).

As has been hinted throughout this chapter, the tension between a subjective response to the music and the idea of a universal communicable meaning manifested in film score conventions thus disappears: they are part of the same mechanism. How an individual interprets the film score Text is entirely dependent on the existence of other Texts: some of these will be familiar to virtually the entire audience (and will therefore be recognized as conventions), while others will be unique to the individual. Furthermore, these Texts change with time: an audience in 1938 was more likely to be familiar with the entire 'Warner Bros.-ian Text' of the 1930s than one watching *The Adventures of Robin Hood* in 2006. This level of familiarity with various Texts that we, as individuals, demonstrate is how we identify conventions.

Korngold, in that sense, is no more or less important than any other member of the audience in creating meaning. He shares the same broad familiarity with these Texts and thus operates within the same cultural framework, recognizing and using conventions. The fact that his scores have attained the status of a 'model' of classical film scoring, then, is perhaps more a reflection of the romantic aesthetic's grip on both film composers and film musicologists (and their need to elevate certain figures as paradigms) than any useful aid to unpicking a score's meanings.

Composers may deliberately collude in the creation of models and even attempt to subvert them in order to mark out their own individualism. While this romantic attitude in composers is understandable, if somewhat limiting, its continued presence in film musicology surely requires challenging. The ostensible tension between an individual and a group response is arguably part of this same romantic aesthetic; however, by recognizing all responses (including the composer's) as both intrinsically unique and yet simultaneously part of a network of Texts capable of sharing enough in common to function on the level of convention, the tension between different types of meaning disappears—as do the notions of models or paradigms. The fact that the individual viewer/listener of *The Adventures of Robin Hood* in 2006 has a unique set of Texts with which s/he is familiar (including films which postdate 1938, for example), merely points to the vast richness of interpretations that are available. The score to *The Adventures of Robin Hood* will thus be continually created anew each time it is experienced.

APPENDIX

Summary of recording information

Serial number	Cue	Date (from Teddy Krise's parts except where indicated). All 1938.
YM 5325-9023-1	"Robin Hood prescore" [written sheet][1]	
YM 5325-9024-1	"Robin Hood prescore" [written sheet]	
YM 5332-9885-3	1E	
YM 5333-9885-5	1E	
YM 5333-9886-1	1F	
YM 5333-9887-3	2A	
YM 5333-9888-3	1C	
YM 5385-9889-6	1D	
YM 5385-9890-2	9A	
YM 5385-9891-3	9B	
YM 5386-9892-1+4	1A	
YM 5386-9893-2+4	1B	
YM 5561-9923-7	8A "bar before #8 to end"	
YM 5659-9920-1-3	2B "#24 to end"	
YM 5659-9921-1[2]	Original 10E	
YM 5660-9921-4[3]	Original 10E	
YM 5660-9922-1	8A "to bar before #8"	
YM 5662-9924-3	8B "to #16"	
YM 5663-9925-3	8B "#16 to end"	
YM 5663-9926-1	Reel 2 timpani insert	
YM 5663-9927-1	"10E trumpets"	

Summary of recording information (continued)

Serial number	Cue	Date
YM 5798-9906-8	"1A Remake"	
YM 5799-9907-6	10B	
YM 5799-9908-1+4	10D	4 March
YM 5800-9909-1	10A	
YM 5800-9910-1	10C	
YM 5800-9911-1	2C "beg to #13"	
YM 5800-9912-2+3	2C "from #13"	
YM 5801-9913-2	2B "beg to #23"	
YM 5806-9933-1	10E "same with chimes"	
YM 5807-9933-2	10E "same with chimes"	
YM 5831-9954-4	3A	
YM 5831-9955-4	3B	
YM 5831-9956-1	3B "#12"	
YM 5832-9957-2	3C	
YM 5832-9958[-]2	3B "whistling"	
YM 5834-9959-6	3D	
YM 5834-9960-2	3E	17 March
YM 5834-9961-1	3F	17 March
YM 5834-9962-3	7A	17 March
YM 5835-9963-6	7B	17 March
YM 5837-9966-1	7C	18 March
YM 5838-9966-3	7C	18 March
YM 5838-9967-1	7D	
YM 5838-9968-1[4]	Trailer Part 1	18 March
YM [5838]-9969-1	Trailer Part 2 [written sheet]	18 March
YM 5838-9969-2	Trailer Part 2	18 March
YM 5838-9970-1	Trailer Part 3	18 March
YM 5839-9971-2	Trailer Part 4	18 March
YM 5839-9972-1	7C "Cymbal"	
YM 5839-9972-1	Trailer Part 2	
YM 5843-9973-2	5A	22 March
YM 5843-9974-2	5C	22 March
YM 5843-9975-3	5D	22 March
YM 5844-9976-2	5B "Ends on down-beat of bar before #5"	22 March
YM 5844-9977-2	5B "from 2 + 3 beats of bar before #5 to #13"	22 March
YM 5844-9978-3	5B "#13 to end"	22 March
YM 5845-9979-5	5E "to #16"	22 March
YM 5846-9980-3	5E "#16 to end"	22 March
YM 5872-23-2+3	6A	
YM 5872-24-2+7	6B	
YM 5873-25-1	6C	
YM 5873-26-5	6D	

Summary of recording information (continued)

Serial number	Cue	Date
YM 5873-27-3+4	6E "to #9"	
YM 5874-28-4	6E "#9 to #17"	
YM 5875-29-5	6E "#17 to end"	
YM 5875-30-2+3	4A	
YM 5875-31-1	4B	
YM 5876-32-5	4C "Beginning to #23B"	
YM 5877-33-4	4C "#23B to 33"	
YM 5877-34-2	4C "#33 to end"	
YM 5877-37-1	6A "Remake fanfare over 1st 4 bars"	
YM 5877-38-2	6A "Same [four bars] cemitone [*sic*] lower (Made Wild)"[5]	
YM 5885-53-7	11A	3 April
YM 5886-54-3	11B	3 April
YM 5886-55-1	11F	3 April
YM 5886-56-3	11C "to #15"	3 April
YM 5887-57-4	11C "#15 to #26"	3 April
YM 5887-58-4+5	11C "#26 to #33"	3 April
YM 5887-59-3	11C "#33 to end"	3 April
YM 5888-60-3	11D "to #7"	3 April
YM 5888s-61-6	11D "#7 to end"	3 April
YM 5889-62-2	11E	Note on back of violin part: "Finished 1st Sunday in April 1938 12.00AM"
YM 5921-116-1	8A "retake (end) Made Wild"	11 April
YM 5921-117-2	9A "last two bars remade (held longer)"	
YM 5922-118-5	10A "revise #1 to #4"	
YM 5922-119-3	10B "#8 to #9 remade"	
YM 5922-120-3	10C "revise"	
YM 5922-121-2+4	10E "(Segue to #6 of 9921)"	11 April

As can be seen, the earliest tracks to be recorded were two items of prescoring (music that would be played on set for actors to mime to). These are probably the songs referred to in the preproduction correspondence that could not be used for legal reasons. The item marked "Reel 2 insert" refers to a piece of paper that reads:

Robin Hood
Reel 2 -
Short (Tympani [sic]) for start of Reel
YM 5663-9926-1

This references a very short timpani and cymbal roll, lasting a second
or so, which was inserted before the beginning of cue 2A. It is not notated in either the full or piano-conductor score, is not found in the percussion part, and obviously postdates the recording of the rest of cue
2A. As can be seen from the table, however, it was added fairly early in
the recording sequence, indicating that the change of mind occurred
while recording was still progressing. The major changes to the score,
in response to the Pomona sneak preview, all occurred at the end of the
sequence, from YM 5921-116-1 to YM 5922-121-1+4, on 11 April
1938.

NOTES

Introduction

1. Brendan Carroll calls the score "one of the finest examples of music wedded to the moving image" in Brendan Carroll, *The Last Prodigy: A Biography of Erich Wolfgang Korngold* (Portland, Ore.: Amadeus Press, 1997), 272–273. Christopher Palmer waxes lyrical about the score in *The Composer in Hollywood* (London: Marion Boyars, 1990), 54–58, and Tony Thomas calls the film "probably the pluperfect example to that time of the blending of film image and music" in his *Music for the Movies*, 2nd ed. (Los Angeles: Silman-James Press, 1997), 176. Also see the discussion of classical film scores in Caryl Flinn, *Strains of Utopia: Gender, Nostalgia and Hollywood Film Music* (Princeton: Princeton University Press, 1992), 108–150, or the analysis of Korngold's score for *Captain Blood* in Kathryn Kalinak, *Settling the Score: Music and the Classical Hollywood Film* (Madison: University of Wisconsin Press, 1992), 66–110. Interestingly, though *The Adventures of Robin Hood* is often praised and assumed to be 'one of the great film scores,' few have examined it in any level of detail.

2. A newspaper poll four years previously had placed him above Schoenberg in a list of the most highly regarded Austrians. The poll was conducted by the *Neues Wiener Tagblatt*. Both Schoenberg (12th) and Korngold (7th) were ranked below Richard Strauss in the arts section. See Carroll, *The Last Prodigy*, 211–212. For a thorough examination of Korngold's critical reception, especially with regard to the operas, see Andreas Giger, "A Matter of Principle: The Consequences for

Korngold's Career," *Journal of Musicology* 16, no. 4 (Autumn 1998): 545–564.

3. See Palmer, *The Composer in Hollywood*, or William Darby and Jack Du Bois, *American Film Music: Major Composers, Techniques, Trends, 1915–1990* (Jefferson, N.C.: McFarland, 1990). Both are organized by devoting chapters to canonic composers.

4. Roland Barthes, "From Work to Text," in *Image, Music, Text: Essays Selected and Translated by Stephen Heath* (London: Fontana Press, 1977), 159.

5. Michael L. Klein, *Intertextuality in Western Art Music* (Bloomington: Indiana University Press, 2005), 111.

Chapter 1

1. These dates do not include Korngold's 1954 involvement with the film *Magic Fire* for which he arranged Wagner's music.

2. Vertically integrated studios had direct control of the three areas of the motion picture industry (production, distribution, and exhibition). Vertical integration was first achieved in the United States by Paramount in 1917, with the other studios following in the 1920s. For an overview of the rise of the vertically integrated studios, see Susan Hayward, *Cinema Studies: The Key Concepts*, 2nd ed. (London: Routledge, 2001), or Douglas Gomery, *The Hollywood Studio System* (Basingstoke: Macmillan, 1986).

3. "Industry to Test Unit Producing to Shave Cost, Improve Quality," *Motion Picture Herald*, 1 August 1931 (104 no. 5), 9.

4. Wallis had replaced Darryl F. Zanuck, who had departed for Twentieth Century-Fox in 1933. Warner Bros. did not adopt the system officially, though, until 1937 when the supervisors were finally given "associate producer" credits.

5. David Bordwell, Janet Staiger, and Kristin Thompson, *The Classical Hollywood Cinema: Film Style and Mode of Production to 1960* (London: Routledge, 1985), 311–319.

6. Lewis Jacobs, *The Rise of the American Film: A Critical History* (New York: Harcourt, Brace, 1939). See also the appendix summarizing American film finance in F. D. Klingender and Stuart Legg, *Money behind the Screen: A Report Prepared on Behalf of the Film Council* (London: Lawrence and Wishart, 1937).

7. Hortense Powdermaker, for example, in her 1946 anthropological study of the studio system, argued that, far from operating with the

smooth precision of an assembly line, Hollywood tended to operate in a constant atmosphere of crisis, reliant on accidental finds from the stage, radio, and literature. See Hortense Powdermaker, *Hollywood, the Dream Factory: An Anthropologist Looks at the Movie-Makers* (London: Secker & Warburg, 1951), 33.

8. André Bazin, "On the 'Politique des auteurs,'" trans. Peter Graham, in *Cahiers du cinéma*, vol. 1, *The 1950s: Neo-Realism, Hollywood, New Wave*, ed. Jim Hillier (London: Routledge, 1985), 258.

9. Thomas Schatz, *The Genius of the System: Hollywood Filmmaking in the Studio Era* (New York: Metro, 1996), 5.

10. See Caryl Flinn, *Strains of Utopia: Gender, Nostalgia and Hollywood Film Music* (Princeton: Princeton University Press, 1992). Flinn points out the importance of placing film music within its social and institutional contexts to avoid cloaking criticism in the "illusion of apparent transcendence" (14). As she points out, "Critics performed rhetorical somersaults in order to transform this industrial product into the document of personal expression, an artifact conceptualized by uniqueness and singularity."(30).

11. Flinn, *Strains of Utopia*, 32–33.

12. Irene Kahn Atkins, *Oral History with Hugo Friedhofer*, American Film Institute/Louis B. Mayer Foundation (unpublished), 129. © 1974 American Film Institute.

13. The notes are dated 10 December 1935. Kathryn Kalinak, *Settling the Score: Music and the Classical Hollywood Film* (Madison: University of Wisconsin Press, 1992), 77.

14. Atkins, *Oral History with Hugo Friedhofer*, 54. © 1974 American Film Institute.

15. Max Steiner, "Scoring the Film," in *We Make the Movies*, ed. Nancy Naumburg (London: Faber & Faber, 1938), 231.

16. See, for example, William Darby and Jack Du Bois, *American Film Music: Major Composers, Techniques, Trends, 1915–1990* (Jefferson, N.C.: McFarland, 1990), xiv. Although postdating the demise of the studio system, Alfred Newman's score for *The Greatest Story Ever Told* (1965) suffered a similar fate to Herrmann's. Cues were dumped in favor of classical extracts and continual rewrites demanded by director George Stevens. Newman tried to have his credit removed, to no avail, prompting David Raksin to christen the debacle "The Saddest Story Ever Told." See Ken Darby's entertaining book *Hollywood Holyland: The Filming and Scoring of* The Greatest Story Ever Told (Metuchen, N.J.: Scarecrow Press, 1992) for an insider's perspective on the 'plight' of the composer.

17. In their book *Composing for the Films*, Adorno and Eisler quote at length from a clause in a typical Hollywood contract: "All material composed, submitted, added or interpolated by the Writer pursuant to this agreement shall automatically become the property of the Corporation, which, for this purpose, shall be deemed the author thereof, the Writer acting entirely as the Corporation's employee…[the Writer grants to the corporation] the right to use, adapt and change the same or any part thereof and to combine the same with other works of the Writer or of any other person to the extent that the Corporation may see fit, including the right to add to, subtract from, arrange, rearrange, revise and adapt such material in any Picture in any manner." They go on to complain that this fluid interpretation of authorship and of the music's status suddenly becomes sharply defined in the event of the composer breaching the contract, such is the omnipotent power of the Corporation over the individual. Then the music is endowed with "peculiar value" and the breach of contract causes the Corporation "irreparable injury and damage." Theodor Adorno and Hanns Eisler, *Composing for the Films*, with a new introduction by Graham McCann (London: Athlone Press, 1994), 55.

18. Randall D. Larson, *Musique Fantastique: A Survey of Film Music in the Fantastic Cinema* (Metuchen, N.J.: Scarecrow Press, 1985), 27.

19. Larson, *Musique Fantastique*, 12.

20. Atkins, *Oral History with Hugo Friedhofer*, 147–153.

21. Luzi Korngold, *Erich Wolfgang Korngold: Ein Lebensbild von Luzi Korngold* (Vienna: Verlag Elisabeth Lafite, 1967), 74.

22. Selznick to O'Shea and Ernest L. Scanlon, 24 July 1947, quoted in Thomas DeMary, "The Mystery of Herrmann's Music for Selznick's *Portrait of Jennie*," *Journal of Film Music* 1, no. 2/3 (Fall–Winter 2003): 162–163.

23. David Raksin, "Holding a Nineteenth Century Pedal at Twentieth Century-Fox," in *Film Music 1*, ed. Clifford McCarty (New York: Garland Publishing, 1989), 173–174.

24. Darby, *Hollywood Holyland*, 190–191.

25. Atkins, *Oral History with Hugo Friedhofer*, 159–160.

26. Roger Parker, *Leonora's Last Act: Essays in Verdian Discourse* (Princeton: Princeton University Press, 1997), 7–8.

27. John McGinness, "From Movement to Moment: Issues of Expression, Form, and Reception in Debussy's *Jeux*," *Cahiers Debussy* 22 (1998): 51–74.

28. See Roland John Wiley, *Tchaikovsky's Ballets: Swan Lake, Sleeping Beauty, Nutcracker* (Oxford: Clarendon Press, 1985), especially the introduction (1–10).

29. Brendan Carroll, *The Last Prodigy: A Biography of Erich Wolfgang Korngold* (Portland, Ore.: Amadeus Press, 1997), 214.

30. Luzi Korngold, *Erich Wolfgang Korngold*, 66–67.

31. Erich Wolfgang Korngold, "Some Experiences in Film Music," *Music and Dance in California*, June 1940, 137.

32. Carroll, *The Last Prodigy*, 240.

33. Julius Korngold, *Die Korngolds in Wien: Der Musikkritiker und das Wunderkind—Aufzeichnungen von Julius Korngold* (Zurich: M&T Verlag, 1991), 123, 129.

34. See *Polykrates* 8 bars before figure 8 to 8.

35. Carroll, *The Last Prodigy*, 218.

Chapter 2

1. Michael Chion, *Audio-Vision: Sound on Screen*, ed. and trans. Claudia Gorbman with a foreword by Walter Murch (New York: Columbia University Press, 1994), 39.

2. Korngold dubbed the 'harpsichord' part himself on thumbtack piano. See Brendan Carroll, *The Last Prodigy: A Biography of Erich Wolfgang Korngold* (Portland, Ore.: Amadeus Press, 1997), 287.

3. Erich Wolfgang Korngold, "Some Experiences in Film Music," *Music and Dance in California*, June 1940, 138.

4. Irene Kahn Atkins, *Oral History with Hugo Friedhofer*, American Film Institute/Louis B. Mayer Foundation, 1974 (unpublished), 65.

5. Atkins, *Oral History with Hugo Friedhofer*, 64.

6. Korngold, "Some Experiences in Film Music," 139.

7. Carroll, *The Last Prodigy*, 303.

8. Atkins, *Oral History with Hugo Friedhofer*, 66. Steiner's use of the click track was probably prompted by his film scoring style, which was more concerned with tying the music to the physical rhythms of the image.

9. Korngold, "Some Experiences in Film Music," 138.

10. See Carroll, *The Last Prodigy*, 275, for discussion of Korngold's favorable contract.

11. Atkins, *Oral History with Hugo Friedhofer*, 75.

12. Korngold, "Some Experiences in Film Music," 138.

13. Atkins, *Oral History with Hugo Friedhofer*, 74.

14. Atkins, *Oral History with Hugo Friedhofer*, 60–61.

15. Letter to Rudy Behlmer of 24 March 1967, quoted in Carroll, *The Last Prodigy*, 251–252.

16. Atkins, *Oral History with Hugo Friedhofer*, 187.

17. The conductor John Mauceri makes this comment on the documentary accompanying *The Adventures of Robin Hood* (Warner Home Video, DVD Region 1, 65131).

18. Quoted in Carroll, *The Last Prodigy*, 258.

19. Tony Thomas, *Music for the Movies*, 2nd ed. (Los Angeles: Silman James Press, 1997), 174.

20. Carroll, *The Last Prodigy*, 281.

21. Carroll, *The Last Prodigy*, 258.

22. See Kate Daubney, *Max Steiner's* Now Voyager: *A Film Score Guide* (Westport, Conn.: Greenwood Press, 2000), 27.

23. Korngold, "Some Experiences in Film Music," 139.

24. This chord is also heard in *Die Kathrin* at figure 294.

25. Interview of 23 May 1926, quoted in Brendan Carroll, "A Musical Guide to the Opera," in *Das Wunder der Heliane*, Decca 436 636-2 (1993), 34.

26. Peter Franklin, "Modernism, Deception, and Musical Others," in *Western Music and Its Others*, ed. Georgina Born and Desmond Hesmondhalgh (Berkeley: University of California Press, 2000), 156.

27. Carroll specifically associates the two (see Carroll, *The Last Prodigy*, 51). The interlocked rising fourths can be found in Act 3 of *Kleider machen Leute* on page 203 of the published vocal score.

28. The death motif also makes an appearance in the Adagio of the Symphony at figure 92 and arguably in the trio of the Scherzo, as well.

29. Atkins, *Oral History with Hugo Friedhofer*, 66.

30. Carroll, *The Last Prodigy*, 252.

31. Theodor Adorno and Hanns Eisler, *Composing for the Films*, with a new introduction by Graham McCann (London: Athlone Press, 1994), 4–6.

32. See "Wotan's Monologue and the Morality of Musical Narration," in Carolyn Abbate, *Unsung Voices: Opera and Musical Narrative in the Nineteenth Century* (Princeton: Princeton University Press, 1991), 156–205.

33. Abbate, *Unsung Voices*, 5.

34. Robbert van der Lek, *Diegetic Music in Opera and Film: A Similarity between Two Genres Analysed in Works by Erich Wolfgang Korngold (1897–1957)* (Amsterdam: Rodopi, 1991), 297.

35. K. J. Donnelly, *The Spectre of Sound: Music in Film and Television* (London: British Film Institute, 2005), 58.

36. Interview with Bruno David Ussher for the *Hollywood Spectator*, in response to a question about why Korngold was not using Tudor or Tudor-inspired music, quoted in Carroll, *The Last Prodigy*, 288.

37. Flinn, *Strains of Utopia*, 108.

38. The use of Franchetti's music for the operatic scene in Paris, on the other hand, seems stylistically entirely inappropriate.

39. Franklin, "Modernism, Deception, and Musical Others," 143–162.

40. The disapproving attitude of Julius Korngold, to whom Erich was always close, could not have failed to evoke some sense of anxiety in the composer.

41. Carroll, *The Last Prodigy*, 290–291.

42. This version was recounted by Ernst Korngold. See Carroll, *The Last Prodigy*, 318–319.

43. Leslie T. Zador and Gregory Rose, "A Conversation with Bernard Herrmann," in *Film Music 1*, ed. Clifford McCarty (New York: Garland Publishers, 1989), 215–216.

44. Carroll, *The Last Prodigy*, 304.

45. Luzi Korngold, *Erich Wolfgang Korngold: Ein Lebensbild von Luzi Korngold* (Vienna: Verlag Elisabeth Lafite, 1967), 47.

46. Carroll, *The Last Prodigy*, 253.

47. For a thorough examination of Korngold's reuse of his film score material in the later concert works, see Robbert van der Lek, "Concert Music as Reused Film Music: E.-W. Korngold's Self-Arrangements," *Acta Musicologica* 66, fasc. 2 (July–Dec., 1994): 78–112.

48. Harold Bloom, *The Anxiety of Influence: A Theory of Poetry* (Oxford: Oxford University Press, 1975).

49. Kevin Korsyn, "Towards a New Poetics of Musical Influence," *Music Analysis* 10, no. 1/2 (March–July 1991): 3–72. Also see Martin Scherzinger, "The 'New Poetics' of Musical Influence: A Response to Kevin Korsyn," *Music Analysis* 13, no. 2/3 (July–Oct. 1994): 298–309, and Lloyd Whitesell, "Men with a Past: Music and the 'Anxiety of Influence,'" *Nineteenth-Century Music* 18, no. 2 (Autumn 1994): 152–167.

50. Korsyn, "Towards a New Poetics of Musical Influence," 46.

51. Christopher Reynolds, *Motives for Allusion* (Cambridge, Mass.: Harvard University Press, 2003).

52. Michael L. Klein, *Intertextuality in Western Art Music* (Bloomington: Indiana University Press, 2005).

53. Klein, *Intertextuality in Western Art Music*, 7–8. One intertextual possibility that Klein does not follow in connection with the Bach C-major prelude is the allusion to the repeated guitar riff opening of the Guns 'n' Roses song "Sweet Child o' Mine" from the album *Appetite for Destruction*. One feels there is potential for even more 'outrageous' assertions here.

54. Carroll, *The Last Prodigy*, 348.

55. The allusion can be heard in the finale at figure 122.

56. Atkins, *Oral History with Hugo Friedhofer*, 122.

57. Tony Thomas mentions the use of a single unnamed tone poem by Liszt for both the duel and the naval battle at the end of the film (Thomas, *Music for the Movies*, 173). Carroll fails to mention any other use of *Prometheus*.

58. See Kathryn Kalinak, *Settling the Score: Music and the Classical Hollywood Film* (Madison: University of Wisconsin Press, 1992), 223.

59. Atkins, *Oral History with Hugo Friedhofer*, 122.

60. The five bars before figure 3 in *Sursum Corda* are squashed together, preserving the rhythmic character and harmony of the original, so that figure 3 of the overture could logically follow the end of this titles sequence, once the on-screen disclaimer that the movie is fiction fades out.

61. Carroll, *The Last Prodigy*, 313.

62. Carroll, *The Last Prodigy*, 286. The section in question can be found eight bars before the first time bar.

63. Carroll, *The Last Prodigy*, 287.

64. Carroll, *The Last Prodigy*, 296.

65. *Juarez* also quotes the Austrian national anthem, while *Anthony Adverse* alludes to "La Marseillaise."

66. The two phrases of the melody are scored for Gershwinesque muted trumpets followed by saxophones.

67. This occurs at 08:38. *The Prince and the Pauper* (Warner Home Video, DVD Region 1, 65227).

68. Kalinak, *Settling the Score*, 91. She mistakenly claims it occurs at the lowering of the French flag.

69. Carroll, *The Last Prodigy*, 263.

70. Carroll, *The Last Prodigy*, 260.

71. Peter Brunette and David Willis, *Screen/Play: Derrida and Film Theory* (Princeton: Princeton University Press, 1989), 88.

72. Found at figure 27 in the published version of the concerto.

73. The concerto also seems to use music from the main title of *Between Two Worlds* at instances like the second bar of figure 58 to figure 60 in the published version.

74. Ruth's music is heard at figure 54.

75. Figure 34.

76. Carroll, *The Last Prodigy*, 320. It is first heard in the viola at figure 67.

77. Carroll, *The Last Prodigy*, 334.

78. Carroll, *The Last Prodigy*, 336.

79. Carroll, *The Last Prodigy*, 348.

80. Carroll, *The Last Prodigy*, 349.

Chapter 3

1. Stephen Knight, ed., *Robin Hood: An Anthology of Scholarship and Criticism* (Woodbridge, Suffolk, England: Brewer, 1999).

2. Joseph Ritson, *Robin Hood: A Collection of all the Ancient Poems, Songs and Ballads, now extant, Relative to that Celebrated English Outlaw*, 1897 edition (London: Routledge, 1997), viii.

3. Ritson, *Robin Hood*, xi.

4. Walter Scott, *Ivanhoe*, edited with an introduction by Graham Tulloch (London: Penguin Classics, 2000), xi.

5. Thomas Love Peacock, *Maid Marian* (London, 1822).

6. Howard Pyle, *The Merry Adventures of Robin Hood of Great Renown in Nottinghamshire As Written and Illustrated by Howard Pyle* (London: Tom Stacey, 1971).

7. Rudy Behlmer, ed., *The Adventures of Robin Hood* (Madison: University of Wisconsin Press, 1979), 11.

8. Behlmer, *The Adventures of Robin Hood*, 17.

9. Behlmer, *The Adventures of Robin Hood*, 17.

10. Behlmer, *The Adventures of Robin Hood*, 18.

11. Behlmer, *The Adventures of Robin Hood*, 24.

12. The USC Warner Bros. Archives, School of Cinematic Arts, University of Southern California, Los Angeles, CA 90089-2211. Production and Research information is found in folders 1495 and 1017.

13. Behlmer, *The Adventures of Robin Hood*, 30.

14. "Warner Bros.," *Fortune* 16, no. 6 (December 1937): 215.

15. Warner Bros. archives, USC.

16. At 0:49:31 in the documentary on the region 1 DVD of *The Adventures of Robin Hood*, a photographed cable mentions that the Pomona sneak preview was on a Thursday. 7 April was the only Thursday between completion of the initial scoring sessions on 3 April and the second sneak preview at the Warner Bros. downtown theater in Los Angeles on 11 April.

17. Behlmer, *The Adventures of Robin Hood*, 35.

18. Warner Bros. archives, USC.

19. Warner Bros. archives, USC.

20. Behlmer, *The Adventures of Robin Hood*, 36.

21. Behlmer, *The Adventures of Robin Hood*, 36.

22. Yvonne Tasker, "Introduction: Action and Adventure Cinema," in *Action and Adventure Cinema*, ed. Yvonne Tasker (London: Routledge, 2004), 2.

23. See José Arroyo, ed., *Action/Spectacle Cinema: A Sight and Sound Reader* (London: British Film Institute, 2000).

24. Tom Ryall, "Genre and Hollywood," in *The Oxford Guide to Film Studies*, ed. John Hill and Pamela Church Gibson (Oxford: Oxford University Press, 1998), 328.

25. Thomas Schatz, *Hollywood Genres: Formulas, Filmmaking, and the Studio System* (Philadelphia: Temple University Press, 1981).

26. Brian Taves, *The Romance of Adventure: The Genre of Historical Adventure Movies* (Jackson: University Press of Mississippi, 1993), 16–17.

27. Taves, *The Romance of Adventure*, 19.

28. Taves, *The Romance of Adventure*, 17.

29. In the Fairbanks version; in *The Adventures of Robin Hood*; and in a 1950 film called *Rogues of Sherwood Forest*.

30. See Barry Norman, *100 Best Films of the Century* (London: Orion, 1998), 62–63. AFI's "100 Years...100 Thrills" listed the film at number 100 (www.afi.com/tvevents/100years/thrills.aspx).

31. Taves, *The Romance of Adventure*, 20.

32. Nick Roddick, *A New Deal in Entertainment: Warner Bros. in the 1930s* (London: British Film Institute, 1983), 241.

33. David A. Gerstner and Janet Staiger, eds., *Authorship and Film: Trafficking with Hollywood* (New York: Routledge, 2003); Virginia Wright Wexman, ed., *Film and Authorship* (New Brunswick, N.J.: Rutgers University Press, 2003).

34. André Bazin, "On the 'Politique des auteurs,'" trans. Peter Graham, in *Cahiers du cinéma*, vol. 1, *The 1950s: Neo-Realism, Hollywood, New Wave*, ed. Jim Hillier (London: Routledge, 1985), 258.

35. Ina Rae Hark, "The Visual Politics of *The Adventures of Robin Hood*," *Journal of Popular Film* 5, no. 1 (1976): 3–17.

36. Schatz, *Hollywood Genres*, 31.

37. Roddick, *A New Deal in Entertainment*, 19. Warner Bros. was the only company other than Loew's to ride out the recession without resorting to bankruptcy or receivership ("Warner Bros.," *Fortune*, 110).

38. Roddick, *A New Deal in Entertainment*, 28.

39. Roddick, *A New Deal in Entertainment*, 64–65.

40. Michael E. Birdwell, *Celluloid Soldiers: The Warner Bros. Campaign against Nazism* (New York: New York University Press, 1999), 10. Harry recommitted himself to Roosevelt in 1940.

41. Roddick, *A New Deal in Entertainment*, 65.

42. Birdwell, *Celluloid Soldiers*, 3.

43. Birdwell, *Celluloid Soldiers*, 66.

44. Birdwell, *Celluloid Soldiers*, 81.

45. Birdwell, *Celluloid Soldiers*, 1.

46. Indeed, the choice of Errol Flynn to play Robin is given added resonance by Flynn's visit to Spain in 1937, where he was rumored to have fought on the side of the loyalists in the Spanish Civil War. See Birdwell, *Celluloid Soldiers*, 31.

47. See, for example, Michael Burleigh, *The Third Reich: A New History* (London: Pan Macmillan, 2001), 318.

48. Hark, "The Visual Politics of *The Adventures of Robin Hood*," 7.

49. John Neubauer, "Overtones of Culture," *Comparative Literature* 51, no. 3 (Summer 1999): 243–254.

50. Lawrence Kramer, *After the Lovedeath: Sexual Violence and the Making of Culture* (Berkeley: University of California Press, 1997), 10.

51. Antonia Quirke, *Jaws* (London: British Film Institute, 2002), 36.

52. Taves, *The Romance of Adventure*, 36.

53. Steve Neale, "Action-Adventure as Hollywood Genre," in Tasker, *Action and Adventure Cinema*, 71–83.

54. Neale, "Action-Adventure as Hollywood Genre," 75.

Chapter 4

1. Warner Bros. archives, USC.

2. Warner Bros. archives, USC.

3. See *Das Echo*, Vienna, 18 May 1937.

4. For a facsimile of the original four-part round, see "Pammelia 74," in Thomas Ravenscroft, *Pammelia, Deutromelia, Melismata,* ed. MacEdward Leach (Philadelphia: American Folklore Society, 1961). A modern edition can be found in Jill Vlasto, "An Elizabethan Anthology of Rounds," *Musical Quarterly* 40, no. 2 (April 1954): 222–234.

5. For a discussion of the sources of this ballad tune, see Claude H. Simpson, *The British Broadside Ballad and Its Music* (New Brunswick, N.J.: Rutgers University Press, 1966), no. 608.

6. William Chappell, *Old English Popular Music,* vol. 1, ed. H. Ellis Wooldridge (London: Chappell, 1893), 273. The tune was harmonized by the editor.

7. On page 215 the editor writes of the tune under discussion: "The notation of the tune is of exactly the same character as that employed in *Summer is icumen in.*"

8. Daubney notes that in twelve years, Korngold wrote thirteen scores, while Steiner managed fifty-five. See Kate Daubney, *Max Steiner's* Now Voyager: *A Film Score Guide* (Westport, Conn.: Greenwood Press, 2000), 9.

9. Brendan Carroll, *The Last Prodigy: A Biography of Erich Wolfgang Korngold* (Portland, Ore.: Amadeus Press, 1997), 269.

10. Carroll, *The Last Prodigy,* 270.

11. Luzi Korngold, *Erich Wolfgang Korngold: Ein Lebensbild von Luzi Korngold* (Vienna: Verlag Elisabeth Lafite, 1967), 77.

12. Warner Bros. archives, USC.

13. Korngold, *Erich Wolfgang Korngold,* 77–78 (translated and quoted in Carroll, *The Last Prodigy,* 271).

14. Korngold, *Erich Wolfgang Korngold,* 64.

15. George Clare, *Last Waltz in Vienna* (London: Pan Books, 2002), 196–197.

16. Indeed, *Captain Blood* would seem to have been a far tougher assignment in terms of time than *Robin Hood.*

17. Irene Kahn Atkins, *Oral History with Hugo Friedhofer,* American Film Institute/Louis B. Mayer Foundation (unpublished), 114. © 1974 American Film Institute.

18. Warner Bros. archives, USC.

19. Sneak previews would no doubt have been done using interlocked projectors (a so-called double-system projection) so that the film could be shown without having to make a composite print with the picture and sound combined on the same piece of film. This would make it easy for any changes to be made to the sound track.

20. Erich Wolfgang Korngold, "Some Experiences in Film Music," *Music and Dance in California*, June 1940, 139.

21. The sketches can be found in the Erich Wolfgang Korngold Collection, Music Division, Library of Congress, box 1, folder 8, "Holograph sketches in pencil."

22. The cue sheets can be found in the Erich Wolfgang Korngold Collection, Music Division, Library of Congress, box 1, folder 8, "Holograph and typescript cue sheets."

23. EWK = Erich Wolfgang Korngold; HWF = Hugo W. Friedhofer; MR = Milan Roder. The short score can be found in the Erich Wolfgang Korngold Collection, Music Division, Library of Congress, box 1, folder 7, "Bound holograph short score in pencil."

24. Carroll, *The Last Prodigy*, 272.

25. *The Adventures of Robin Hood*, Marco Polo 8.225268 liner notes, 12.

26. Email correspondence with Brendan Carroll, 26 August 2004.

27. The inserted section in cue 7A is written on a green manuscript paper of a different type than is used by Friedhofer or Roder. Though the handwriting is similar to Roder's, it could be Bassett's. Nevertheless, this section does not orchestrate any new music, as Roder's note indicates ("copy 24 bars of no. 2-B from [figures] 1 to 6"), but merely copies out a few lines for the conductor. It is just as likely, therefore, that this is the hand of one of the copyists.

28. Atkins, *Oral History with Hugo Friedhofer*, 42–45, 136, 148.

29. Atkins, *Oral History with Hugo Friedhofer*, 57–58.

30. An example of this can be found in cue 3B. Three bars before figure 3, the piano-conductor score marks harmonics for the solo violin's A's. This is not in Korngold's original and must have been obtained from the full score.

31. Robbert van der Lek, *Diegetic Music in Opera and Film: A Similarity between Two Genres Analysed in Works by Erich Wolfgang Korngold (1897–1957)* (Amsterdam: Rodopi, 1991), 189.

32. EWK = Erich Wolfgang Korngold; HWF = Hugo W. Friedhofer; MR = Milan Roder. The full score can be found in the Warner Bros. archives, USC, box numbers 15–17, folder number 1243.

33. Generally with a serial number at the bottom of the page of either "2500-6-37-K-I Co." or "5M-2-38-K-I-Co."

34. Atkins, *Oral History with Hugo Friedhofer*, 125.

35. *Captain Blood: Classic Film Scores for Errol Flynn*, National Philharmonic Orchestra/Charles Gerhardt, RCA Victor 0912.

36. Information comes from a memo from Robert Taplinger to Walter MacEwen sent on 11 May, Warner Bros. archives, USC.

37. Carroll, *The Last Prodigy*, 273.

38. Carroll, *The Last Prodigy*, 273.

39. Carroll, *The Last Prodigy*, 273.

40. Carroll, *The Last Prodigy*, 404.

41. See liner notes for *The Adventures of Robin Hood*, Marco Polo 8.225268, 24.

42. For its New York performance in 1922, Korngold provided his own program note that explained the title was meant to suggest "a mood of struggle and aspiration, a joyous deliverance out of storm and stress." See Carroll, *The Last Prodigy*, 159.

43. Luzi Korngold, *Erich Wolfgang Korngold*, 32. The rest of the program consisted of Beethoven's *Egmont Overture*, a Leopold Mozart symphony, Mahler's *Kindertotenlieder*, Korngold's *Much Ado about Nothing* Suite, and the *Vorspiel* from *Violanta*.

44. Julius Korngold, *Die Korngolds in Wien: Der Musikkritiker und das Wunderkind—Aufzeichnungen von Julius Korngold* (Zurich: M&T Verlag, 1991), 265.

45. At figure 11 in 8A, the start of the second section of material taken from *Sursum Corda*, Friedhofer copied slurs in 1st clarinet and bass clarinet. While these make perfect sense in the context of *Sursum Corda*, they are clearly erroneous coming after the newly composed material in 8A. The mistake undoubtedly happened because there is a page turn in both scores at this point.

46. Carroll, *The Last Prodigy*, 205. Korngold was given the sketches by Fall's widow and asked to finish the work by Hubert Marischka.

47. The rather unusual pseudo-German/English title of the waltz also hold true for the other sections in the "beauty contest of nations": Miß Britannia; Miß Slavia; Miß Honolulu; Miß Germania; Miß Italia, Hispania, France; Miß Scandinavia; and Miß America.

48. See Carroll, *The Last Prodigy*, 293.

49. See *The Adventures of Robin Hood*, Marco Polo 8.225268, 13.

50. *Captain Blood*, available in a double bill with *The Adventures of Robin Hood* on VHS S035589, is significantly cut.

51. See Rudy Behlmer, ed., *The Adventures of Robin Hood* (Madison: University of Wisconsin Press, 1979), 38–39. However, how we see *The Adventures of Robin Hood* can make quite a difference to the way we perceive its music. The quality of the sound in a 1938 cinema print, or a VHS copy of the film, must surely differ from that experi-

enced in a 'cleaned-up' DVD release. Previously unheard nuances in orchestrational detail, for example, may suddenly become clear.

52. For an extensive discussion of the various changes and revisions made to the score, see Benjamin John Winters, *Korngold's Merry Men: Music and Authorship in the Hollywood Studio System* (D.Phil. diss., Oxford University, 2005).

53. Cue 8A was also subtly altered by the process of 'sweetening.' A harp glissando was added in the third bar of figure 8 (where Robin's men attack the guards at Nottingham gate), though there is nothing in the full score or parts to indicate this. Sabaneev discusses the mixing of two musical records, which may have occurred here. "This permits of a certain amount of retouching in the orchestration; for instance, percussion instruments previously omitted may be added. Then the percussion background is filmed separately, and afterwards mixed." Leonid Sabaneev, *Music for the Films: A Handbook for Composers and Conductors*, trans. S. W. Pring (London: Sir Isaac Pitman & Sons, 1935), 120. Similarly, extra chords were added to parallel Robin's on-screen 'hacks' at the rope holding the portcullis of Nottingham gate. Four of these sword chops were initially in place in the full score and recorded normally (as can be heard in the audio-only track of the DVD); however, at some point, two extra musical chops were added. It has to be a distinct possibility that the two previous recorded bars were dubbed over the existing YM 5561-9923-7 in a clear example of sweetening. This change could therefore be achieved without recalling the orchestra. As no changes have been made in the full score at this point, and it appears from listening to the film that the rest of the orchestra is playing underneath these extra chops, this seems the most likely explanation.

54. Milton Lustig, *Music Editing for the Motion Pictures* (New York: Hastings House, 1980), 160–163. This technique requires the chord to be sustained in the first place so that a loop can be made. Sabaneev also discusses the lengthening of music: "If the music is continuous and has no pauses, it may be lengthened by pasting new frames (countertypes of those adjoining) into the sustained passages...in music of any kind we usually have moments in which the change of sounds is retarded, and here we can always find a so-called stable frame, i.e. one in which the figure of vibrations is constant throughout. A skilled *montagist* can detect this with the naked eye, or by means of a magnifying glass. From a frame of this kind a countertype or countertypes are prepared and pasted in, thereby prolonging the passage." Sabaneev, *Music for the Films*, 110–111.

55. See Caryl Flinn, *Strains of Utopia: Gender, Nostalgia, and Hollywood Film Music* (Princeton: Princeton University Press, 1992), 33.

Chapter 5

1. Edward T. Cone, *The Composer's Voice* (Berkeley: University of California Press, 1974), 13.

2. Roland Barthes, *S/Z: An Essay*, trans. Richard Miller (New York: Hill & Wang, 1974).

3. Roland Barthes, *The Pleasure of the Text*, trans. Richard Miller (New York: Hill & Wang, 1975), 10–12.

4. Indeed the DVD revolution has provided us with a text that is closer to the written literary text than anything the cinema can manage: we can pause, fast-forward, rewind, skip to a different chapter, and dip in and out in a way that encourages Barthes's rereading of a text.

5. Lawrence Kramer, "The Musicology of the Future," *Repercussions* 1 (1992): 10.

6. See Lawrence Kramer, *Musical Meaning: Toward a Critical History* (Berkeley: University of California Press, 2002).

7. Kramer, *Musical Meaning*, 162.

8. Kramer, *Musical Meaning*, 284–286.

9. Kramer's writing style in *Musical Meaning* is also stridently personal. On page 266, for example, he writes: "I would like to bury the concept of a constitutive originality, an originality synonymous with seriousness and 'greatness' in art. If I could have my way, I would bury it so deep it could never return."

10. Indeed, this theme is labeled "Robin Hood Hero" in the piano-conductor score.

11. Similarly, the retake end to cue 8A recorded on 11 April featured the disjunct motion; the version heard in the film, however, does not (see example 4.16).

12. Raymond Monelle, *The Sense of Music: Semiotic Essays* (Princeton: Princeton University Press, 2000), 45–65.

13. Monelle, *The Sense of Music*, 49–53.

14. It is much like the dinner scene aboard the *Albatross* in *The Sea Hawk* in function and tone, though completely different in style.

15. Korngold's care to avoid drowning out the dialogue might provide a more practical reason.

16. In *Devotion*, the sight of Branwell's caricature sketches is suddenly matched by comic muted trombones, as if the score is offering the listener a musical equivalent of the artist's opinion of his sitter.

17. See Michel Chion, *Audio-Vision: Sound on Screen*, ed. and trans. Claudia Gorbman (New York: Columbia University Press, 1994), 73–82.

18. Anahid Kassabian, *Hearing Film: Tracking Identifications in Contemporary Hollywood Film Music* (New York: Routledge, 2001), 42–49.

19. The harmonic sequences are reminiscent of the title music from *Another Dawn*.

20. "Geffaster Abschied" from Korngold's *Abschiedslieder* also bears a striking resemblance to "Das himmlische Leben," though the singer's opening phrase begins with a rising minor seventh rather than the major sixth of the Mahler.

21. *Sursum Corda* (meaning "lift up your hearts") is part of the text of the Eucharist in the Christian liturgy.

22. See Edward Said, *Orientalism* (Harmondsworth, England: Penguin, 1995), and Lawrence Kramer, "From the Other to the Abject," in *Classical Music: Postmodern Knowledge* (Berkeley: University of California Press, 1995), 33–66.

23. See, for example, Jeffrey Perry, "The Wanderer's Many Returns: Schubert's Variations Reconsidered," *Journal of Musicology* 19, no. 2 (Spring 2002): 374–416.

24. At all points, music could be said to be 'intertextually unstable,' since it has the capacity to move along any of a huge number of possible paths.

25. In Gorbman's terminology, "spectacle bonding" is occurring here. See Claudia Gorbman, *Unheard Melodies: Narrative Film Music* (Bloomington: Indiana University Press, 1987), 68. We could also see this moment as an example of one of Barbara Klinger's "digressions." See Barbara Klinger, "Digressions at the Cinema: Reception and Mass Culture," *Cinema Journal* 28, no. 4 (Summer 1989): 3–19.

26. See figure 34. Its harmonic instability is created through the descending chromatic.

27. See Michael L. Klein, *Intertextuality in Western Art Music* (Bloomington: Indiana University Press, 2005), 4–5.

28. *Essential War Epic Collection: A Bridge Too Far; Battle of Britain; The Great Escape* (MGM Home Entertainment, DVD Region 2, 10001266).

Appendix

1. "Written sheet" refers to pages included in the piano-conductor score that contain no music.

2. Information comes from a copy of the piano-conductor score stored with orchestral parts.

3. Information comes from a copy of the piano-conductor score stored with orchestral parts.

4. This information, including the date, comes from the copy of the piano-conductor score stored with the orchestral parts. Teddy Krise's parts for trailers 1, 3 and 4 also confirm the date information.

5. A recording "made wild" was done without any reference to the image. Exact synchronization of music and image could not be guaranteed, so the technique could be used only for short passages.

BIBLIOGRAPHY

Abbate, Carolyn. *Unsung Voices: Opera and Musical Narrative in the Nineteenth Century.* Princeton: Princeton University Press, 1991.

Adorno, Theodor, and Hanns Eisler. *Composing for the Films.* With a new introduction by Graham McCann. London: Athlone Press, 1994.

American Film Institute. "100 Years...100 Thrills," www.afi.com/tvevents/100years/thrills.aspx

Arroyo, José, ed. *Action/Spectacle Cinema: A Sight and Sound Reader.* London: British Film Institute, 2000.

Atkins, Irene Kahn. *Oral History: Hugo Friedhofer interviewed by Irene Kahn Atkins, March 13–April 29, 1974.* American Film Institute/Louis B. Mayer Foundation.

Barthes, Roland. "The Death of the Author." 142–148 in *Image, Music, Text: Essays Selected and Translated by Stephen Heath.* London: Fontana Press, 1977.

————."From Work to Text." 155–164 in *Image, Music, Text: Essays Selected and Translated by Stephen Heath.* London: Fontana Press, 1977.

————. *The Pleasure of the Text,* translated by Richard Miller. Oxford: Blackwell, 1990.

————. *S/Z: An Essay,* translated by Richard Miller. New York: Hill & Wang, 1974.

Bazin, André. "On the 'Politique des auteurs.'" 248–259 in *Cahiers du cinéma,* vol. 1, *The 1950s: Neo-Realism, Hollywood, New Wave,* edited by Jim Hillier. London: Routledge, 1985.

Behlmer, Rudy. *Behind the Scenes: The making of—*. Hollywood: Samuel French, 1990.

———, ed. *The Adventures of Robin Hood*. Madison: University of Wisconsin Press, 1979.

Birdwell, Michael E. *Celluloid Soldiers: The Warner Bros. Campaign against Nazism*. New York: New York University Press, 1999.

Bloom, Harold. *The Anxiety of Influence: A Theory of Poetry*. Oxford: Oxford University Press, 1975.

Bordwell, David, Janet Staiger, and Kristin Thompson. *The Classical Hollywood Cinema: Film Style and Mode of Production to 1960*. London: Routledge & Kegan Paul, 1985.

Brunette, Peter, and David Willis. *Screen/Play: Derrida and Film Theory*. Princeton: Princeton University Press, 1989.

Burleigh, Michael. *The Third Reich: A New History*. London: Pan Macmillan, 2001.

Carroll, Brendan G. *The Last Prodigy: A Biography of Erich Wolfgang Korngold*. Portland, Ore.: Amadeus Press, 1997.

———. "A Musical Guide to the Opera." 34–38 in *Das Wunder der Heliane*, Decca 436 636-2 (1993).

Chappell, William. *Old English Popular Music*, vol. 1, edited by H. Ellis Wooldridge. London: Chappell, 1893.

Chion, Michael. *Audio-Vision: Sound on Screen*, edited and translated by Claudia Gorbman with a foreword by Walter Murch. New York: Columbia University Press, 1994.

Clare, George. *Last Waltz in Vienna*. London: Pan Books, 2002.

Cone, Edward T. *The Composer's Voice*. Berkeley: University of California Press, 1974.

Darby, Ken. *Hollywood Holyland: The Filming and Scoring of* The Greatest Story Ever Told. Filmmakers series no. 30. Metuchen, N.J.: Scarecrow Press, 1992.

Darby, William, and Jack Du Bois. *American Film Music: Major Composers, Techniques, Trends, 1915–1990*. Jefferson, N.C.: McFarland, 1990.

Daubney, Kate. *Max Steiner's* Now, Voyager: *A Film Score Guide*. Westport, Conn.: Greenwood Press, 2000.

DeMary, Thomas. "The Mystery of Herrmann's Music for Selznick's *Portrait of Jennie*." *Journal of Film Music* 1, no. 2/3 (Fall–Winter 2003): 153–183.

Donnelly, K. J. *The Spectre of Sound: Music in Film and Television*. London: British Film Institute, 2005.

Flinn, Caryl. *Strains of Utopia: Gender, Nostalgia and Hollywood Film Music*. Princeton: Princeton University Press, 1992.

Franklin, Peter. "Modernism, Deception, and Musical Others." 143–162 in *Western Music and Its Others*, edited by Georgina Born and Desmond Hesmondhalgh. Berkeley: University of California Press, 2000.

Gerstner, David A., and Janet Staiger, eds. *Authorship and Film: Trafficking with Hollywood*. New York: Routledge, 2003.

Giger, Andreas. "A Matter of Principle: The Consequences for Korngold's Career." *Journal of Musicology* 16, no. 4 (Autumn 1998): 545–564.

Gomery, Douglas. *The Hollywood Studio System*. Basingstoke, England: Macmillan, 1986.

Gorbman, Claudia. *Unheard Melodies: Narrative Film Music*. Bloomington: Indiana University Press, 1987.

Hark, Ina Rae. "The Visual Politics of *The Adventures of Robin Hood*." *Journal of Popular Film* 5, no. 1 (1976): 3–17.

Hayward, Susan. *Cinema Studies: The Key Concepts*. 2nd ed. London: Routledge, 2001.

"Industry to Test Unit Producing to Shave Cost, Improve Quality." *Motion Picture Herald* 104, no. 5 (1 August 1931).

Jacobs, Lewis. *The Rise of the American Film: A Critical History*. New York: Harcourt, Brace, 1939.

Kalinak, Kathryn. *Settling the Score: Music and the Classical Hollywood Film*. Madison: University of Wisconsin Press, 1992.

Kassabian, Anahid. *Hearing Film: Tracking Identifications in Contemporary Hollywood Film Music*. New York: Routledge, 2001.

Klein, Michael L. *Intertextuality in Western Art Music*. Bloomington: Indiana University Press, 2005.

Klingender, F. D., and Stuart Legg. *Money behind the Screen: A Report Prepared on Behalf of the Film Council*. London: Lawrence and Wishart, 1937.

Klinger, Barbara. "Digressions at the Cinema: Reception and Mass Culture." *Cinema Journal* 28, no. 4 (Summer 1989): 3–19.

Knight, Stephen, ed. *Robin Hood: An Anthology of Scholarship and Criticism*. Woodbridge, Suffolk, England: Brewer, 1999.

Korngold, Erich Wolfgang. "Some Experiences in Film Music." *Music and Dance in California*, June 1940: 137–139.

Korngold, Julius. *Die Korngolds in Wien: Der Musikkritiker und das Wunderkind—Aufzeichnungen von Julius Korngold*. Zurich: M&T Verlag, 1991.

Korngold, Luzi. *Erich Wolfgang Korngold: Ein Lebensbild von Luzi Korngold.* Vienna: Verlag Elisabeth Lafite, 1967.

Korsyn, Kevin. "Towards a New Poetics of Musical Influence." *Music Analysis* 10, no. 1/2 (March–July 1991): 3–72.

Kramer, Lawrence. *After the Lovedeath: Sexual Violence and the Making of Culture.* Berkeley: University of California Press, 1997.

———. *Classical Music: Postmodern Knowledge.* Berkeley: University of California Press, 1995.

———. *Musical Meaning: Toward a Critical History.* Berkeley: University of California Press, 2002.

———. "The Musicology of the Future." *Repercussions* 1 (1992): 5–18.

Larson, Randall D. *Musique Fantastique: A Survey of Film Music in the Fantastic Cinema.* Metuchen, N.J.: Scarecrow Press, 1985.

Lek, Robbert van der. "Concert Music as Reused Film Music: E.-W. Korngold's Self-Arrangements." *Acta Musicologica* 66, fasc. 2 (July–Dec., 1994): 78–112.

———. *Diegetic Music in Opera and Film: A Similarity between Two Genres Analysed in Works by Erich Wolfgang Korngold (1897–1957).* Amsterdam: Rodopi, 1991.

Lustig, Milton. *Music Editing for the Motion Pictures.* New York: Hastings House, 1980.

McGinness, John. "From Movement to Moment: Issues of Expression, Form, and Reception in Debussy's *Jeux.*" *Cahiers Debussy* 22 (1998): 51–74.

Monelle, Raymond. *The Sense of Music: Semiotic Essays.* Princeton: Princeton University Press, 2000.

Neale, Steve. "Action-Adventure as Hollywood Genre." 71–83 in *Action and Adventure Cinema*, edited by Yvonne Tasker. London: Routledge, 2004.

Neubauer, John. "Overtones of Culture." *Comparative Literature* 51, no. 3 (Summer 1999): 243–254.

Norman, Barry. *100 Best Films of the Century.* London: Orion, 1998.

Palmer, Christopher. *The Composer in Hollywood.* London: Marion Boyars, 1990.

Parker, Roger. *Leonora's Last Act: Essays in Verdian Discourse.* Princeton: Princeton University Press, 1997.

Peacock, Thomas Love. *Maid Marian.* London, 1822.

Perry, Jeffrey. "The Wanderer's Many Returns: Schubert's Variations Reconsidered." *Journal of Musicology* 19, no. 2 (Spring 2002): 374–416.

Powdermaker, Hortense. *Hollywood, the Dream Factory: An Anthropologist Looks at the Movie-Makers.* London: Secker & Warburg, 1951.

Pyle, Howard. *The Merry Adventures of Robin Hood of Great Renown in Nottinghamshire As Written and Illustrated by Howard Pyle.* London: Tom Stacey, 1971.

Quirke, Antonia. *Jaws.* BFI Modern Classics. London: British Film Institute, 2002.

Raksin, David. "Holding a Nineteenth-Century Pedal at Twentieth Century-Fox." 167–181 in *Film Music 1*, edited by Clifford McCarty. New York: Garland Publishing, 1989.

Ravenscroft, Thomas. *Pammelia, Deutromelia, Melismata*, edited by MacEdward Leach. Philadelphia: American Folklore Society, 1961.

Reynolds, Christopher. *Motives for Allusion.* Cambridge, Mass.: Harvard University Press, 2003.

Ritson, Joseph. *Robin Hood: A Collection of all the Ancient Poems, Songs and Ballads, now extant, Relative to that Celebrated English Outlaw.* 1897 edition. London: Routledge, 1997.

Roddick, Nick. *A New Deal in Entertainment: Warner Bros. in the 1930s.* London: British Film Institute, 1983.

Ryall, Tom. "Genre and Hollywood." 327–338 in *The Oxford Guide to Film Studies*, edited by John Hill and Pamela Church Gibson. Oxford: Oxford University Press, 1998.

Sabaneev, Leonid. *Music for the Films: A Handbook for Composers and Conductors*, translated by S. W. Pring. London: Sir Isaac Pitman & Sons, 1935.

Said, Edward. *Orientalism.* Harmondsworth, England: Penguin, 1995.

Schatz, Thomas. *The Genius of the System: Hollywood Filmmaking in the Studio Era.* New York: Metro, 1996.

———. *Hollywood Genres: Formulas, Filmmaking, and the Studio System.* Philadelphia: Temple University Press, 1981.

Scherzinger, Martin. "The 'New Poetics' of Musical Influence: A Response to Kevin Korsyn." *Music Analysis* 13, no. 2/3 (July–Oct. 1994): 298–309.

Scott, Walter. *Ivanhoe*, edited with an introduction by Graham Tulloch. London: Penguin Classics, 2000.

Simpson, Claude H. *The British Broadside Ballad and Its Music.* New Brunswick, N.J.: Rutgers University Press, 1966.

Steiner, Max. "Scoring the Film." 216–238 in *We Make the Movies*, edited by Nancy Naumburg. London: Faber & Faber, 1938.

Tasker, Yvonne, ed. *Action and Adventure Cinema*. London: Routledge, 2004.

Taves, Brian. *The Romance of Adventure: The Genre of Historical Adventure Movies*. Jackson: University Press of Mississippi, 1993.

Thomas, Tony. *Music for the Movies*. 2nd ed. Los Angeles: Silman James Press, 1997.

Vlasto, Jill. "An Elizabethan Anthology of Rounds." *Musical Quarterly* 40, no. 2 (April 1954): 222–234.

"Warner Bros." *Fortune* 16, no. 6 (December 1937): 110–113+.

Wexman, Virginia Wright, ed. *Film and Authorship*. New Brunswick, N.J.: Rutgers University Press, 2003.

Whitesell, Lloyd. "Men with a Past: Music and the 'Anxiety of Influence.'" *Nineteenth-Century Music* 18, no. 2 (Autumn 1994): 152–167.

Wiley, Roland John. *Tchaikovsky's Ballets: Swan Lake, Sleeping Beauty, Nutcracker*. Oxford: Clarendon Press, 1985.

Winters, Benjamin John. *Korngold's Merry Men: Music and Authorship in the Hollywood Studio System*. D.Phil. diss., Oxford University, 2005.

Zador, Leslie T., and Gregory Rose. "A Conversation with Bernard Herrmann." 209–253 in *Film Music 1*, edited by Clifford McCarty. New York: Garland Publishers, 1989.

INDEX

ABOUT THE AUTHOR

Ben Winters completed his doctorate at the University of Oxford and is currently a research fellow in musicology at City University, London. He has taught at the universities of Oxford and Bristol and has contributed to the forthcoming *Cambridge Companion to Film Music*.

Printed in Great Britain
by Amazon